PENNSYLVANIA TEST PREP

PSSA Practice Book

English Language Arts

Grade 5

© 2015 by Test Master Press Pennsylvania

All rights reserved. No part of this book may be reproduced or transmitted in any form or by any means, electronic, mechanical, photocopying, recording, or otherwise without prior written permission.

ISBN 978-1519304117

CONTENTS

PSSA Practice Book, English Language Arts, Grade 5

Introduction		**4**
PSSA English Language Arts Practice Sets		**5**
Set 1	Reading: Literary Text	5
Set 2	Reading: Literary Text	14
Set 3	Reading: Informational Text	22
Set 4	Reading: Informational Text	30
Set 5	Reading and Writing: Literary Text with Writing Task	37
Set 6	Reading and Writing: Literary Text with Writing Task	46
Set 7	Language: Writing and Editing Tasks	55
Set 8	Writing: Opinion Piece Writing Task	64
Set 9	Reading and Writing: Informational Text with Writing Task	68
Set 10	Reading and Writing: Literary Text with Writing Task	79
Set 11	Reading and Writing: Informational Text with Writing Task	88
Set 12	Reading and Writing: Informational Text with Writing Task	100
Set 13	Reading and Writing: Literary Text with Writing Task	109
Set 14	Reading and Writing: Informational Text with Writing Task	118
Set 15	Language: Writing and Editing Tasks	129
Set 16	Writing: Informative/Explanatory Writing Task	138
Set 17	Reading and Writing: Informational Texts with Writing Task	142
Set 18	Reading and Writing: Literary Texts with Writing Task	156
Set 19	Reading and Writing: Literary Texts with Writing Task	170
Set 20	Reading and Writing: Informational Texts with Writing Task	187
Extras		**203**
	Answer Key	203
	Informative/Explanatory Writing Rubric	230
	Opinion Writing Rubric	231
	Text-Dependent Analysis Writing Rubric	232
	Narrative Writing Rubric	233

INTRODUCTION
For Parents, Teachers, and Tutors

About the PSSA English Language Arts Tests

Students are assessed each year by taking the PSSA English Language Arts test. The tests cover reading of literature texts, reading of informational texts, writing, and language. This book contains practice sets that will prepare students for the PSSA assessments. The practice sets cover all the skills assessed and provide practice with the types of questions and tasks found on the real assessments.

Key Features of the PSSA English Language Arts Tests

The PSSA English Language Arts tests have key features that students will need to be familiar with. There are certain skills emphasized on the test, as well as new question styles and formats. This book has been developed to prepare students for all the key features listed below.

- The tests assess reading, writing, and language skills.
- There is a greater emphasis on writing skills. Students will have to provide more written answers, as well as write informative/explanatory essays, opinion pieces, and narratives.
- The tests includes text-dependent analysis questions. In these questions, students write an essay in response to a passage or a set of passages.
- There are evidence-based selected-response questions, where a first question asks about a text, and a second question expands on the first by asking for evidence.
- There is a strong focus on close reading and using evidence from the texts. Questions will require students to read texts closely and to use specific evidence from the text.
- There is a greater focus on analysis and evaluation. Instead of only showing they comprehend texts, students will be asked questions that require them to analyze a text closely, evaluate a text, relate to a text, or form and support an opinion about a text.

Completing the Practice Sets

This practice book is divided into convenient practice sets that will give students experience with all the tasks they will need to complete on the real PSSA tests. The first sets focus on reading, and then more complex tasks are introduced in the following sets. The sets include multiple-choice questions like those found on the test. The sets also include open-response questions that will encourage students to analyze texts closely, help develop strong reading comprehension skills, and provide practice writing in response to passages. The writing tasks in the book will prepare students for the text-dependent analysis questions as well as the writing prompts.

By completing all the practice sets, students will develop all the English Language Arts skills they need and become familiar with all the tasks they will encounter on the real assessments.

About the Pennsylvania Core Standards

All the questions on the PSSA tests are based on the skills listed in the Pennsylvania Core Standards. The answer key at the back of the book lists the specific skill covered by each question.

PSSA English Language Arts

Practice Set 1

Reading

Literary Text

Instructions

This set has one passage for you to read. The passage is followed by questions.

Read each question carefully. For each multiple-choice question, fill in the circle for the correct answer. For other types of questions, follow the instructions given. Some of the questions require a written answer. Write your answer on the lines provided.

The Lighthouse

Simon was fascinated with the lighthouse to the south of the island. It was just two miles from his front door. The lighthouse stood proudly above the sea and cast its light for miles. It had stood in that spot for over two hundred years. Wind and rain had battered it, but the lighthouse stood strong and sturdy. During the day, you could see the aging of the old stone bricks.

Simon often stared at the lighthouse and wondered about its history. He had even heard rumors that it was haunted by a stonemason that had helped build it. He had been told the stonemason's initials were carved into some of the stones. Simon had never been close enough to see it for himself. At night it was an eerie presence. The white stones shone in the moonlight like a ghost hovering over the sea. Simon knew the lighthouse was meant to protect sailors. But sometimes he felt like it was watching him. Simon and his friends were scared to even go near it.

One night, Rick was staying at Simon's house. Just like Simon, he couldn't help stare at the lighthouse.

"I think we should head over there," said Rick, who was Simon's best friend. He was always more adventurous than his sensible friend.

Simon thought carefully before responding.

"But aren't you scared?" he asked.

"Not at all. Are you?" Rick replied.

Simon did not want to look scared in front of his best friend.

"No," he replied nervously.

"That is settled then," said Rick. "We will head out this evening."

After dinner, they gathered some food and supplies and packed them into Rick's backpack. Then they headed out toward the lighthouse. Both boys were very quiet as they walked through the fields on the island.

"You're not saying much," said Simon. "Are you okay?"

"I'm fine," said Rick. "I was just thinking."

When they reached the shore, the sun was starting to set above the sea. The boys slowly climbed the small rock face as the sun went down. They both stopped as they stood in front of the lighthouse door.

"In you go then Simon," said Rick, gesturing toward the wooden door.

"You go first," said Simon. "It was your idea."

Rick paused and didn't say a single word. Then Rick edged toward the door. He stopped and looked back at Simon, who gave a small nod of encouragement. He arrived at the step and reached out for the door handle. Simon had stayed back in the shadows. As Rick twisted the handle, he suddenly heard a loud growling from inside.

"Run!" shouted Rick at the top of his voice.

He raced away, with Simon following close behind him. They ran back to the main road and headed back toward Simon's house. Rick looked very sheepish as they made their way home.

"Didn't you want to see inside?" asked Simon.

Rick shrugged and looked down at the ground.

"I guess it was scarier than I thought," he whispered.

"Oh, I don't know," said Simon. "It wasn't that bad."

1. Read this sentence from the passage.

   At night it was an eerie presence.

   Circle **all** the words that have about the same meaning as <u>eerie</u>.

   (creepy)   amusing   (ghostly)   useful

   gigantic   (scary)   calming   welcoming

2. Select the **three** details given about the lighthouse that best explain why Simon finds it eerie. Tick **three** boxes to show your choices.

   ☐ Simon is fascinated by it.

   ☐ It is two miles from Simon's house.

   ☐ It stands proudly above the sea.

   ☐ It casts its light for miles.

   ☑ It is two hundred years old.

   ☐ It is made of white stones that seem to shine at night.

   ☑ There are rumors that it is haunted.

   ☐ Simon has never been near it.

   ☐ Its job is to protect sailors.

   ☑ Simon feels like it is watching him.

3. Read this sentence from the passage.

Then Rick edged toward the door.

The word <u>edged</u> shows that Rick moved –

- Ⓐ swiftly
- Ⓑ slowly
- Ⓒ suddenly
- Ⓓ smoothly

4. Based on your answer to Question 3, what does the way Rick moves show about how he feels? Use details from the passage in your answer.

The way Rick moved shows that he is feeling scared to go inside. Since Simon told him to go in first since it was his idea, he had to go in but didn't want to since he was scared. This is why he slowly went.

5. Which statement is most likely true about Rick?

    Ⓐ He is not scared of anything.

    Ⓑ He is not as fearless as he says he is.

    Ⓒ He enjoys seeing how scared Simon is.

    Ⓓ He only pretends to be frightened.

6. Which word in the sentence below shows that the author is using personification?

    The lighthouse stood proudly above the sea and cast its light for miles.

    Ⓐ *proudly*

    Ⓑ *above*

    Ⓒ *light*

    Ⓓ *miles*

7. Why does Rick tell Simon to run?

    Ⓐ He sees a creature inside the lighthouse.

    Ⓑ He hears a noise from inside the lighthouse.

    Ⓒ He thinks they are going to get in trouble for being inside the lighthouse.

    Ⓓ He realizes that the owner of the lighthouse is home.

8. At the start of the passage, Rick says that he is not scared of going to the lighthouse. Describe **two** details that suggest that Rick is more scared than he admits.

1: _In the story, Rick heard a sound and yelled, "Run!" This shows that he was scared of the noise and wanted to go._

2: _The Author states, "I guess it was scarier than I thought." This tells us he admits to it being scary._

9. What is the point of view in the passage?
   - Ⓐ First person
   - Ⓑ Second person
   - Ⓒ Third person limited
   - Ⓓ Third person omniscient

10. According to the passage, how is Simon different from Rick?
    - Ⓐ He is more sensible.
    - Ⓑ He is more adventurous.
    - Ⓒ He is more intelligent.
    - Ⓓ He is more determined.

11. Read this sentence from the passage.

   Rick shrugged and looked down at the ground.

   The author uses this description to suggest that Rick feels —

   Ⓐ angry
   ⬤ embarrassed
   Ⓒ amused
   Ⓓ terrified

12. Circle the word below that you think best describes Simon. Explain why you made that choice.

   brave   (cowardly)

   I think Simon is more cowardly than brave. I know this because he seemed scared to go to the lighthouse. He is also not that adventurous which shows he may be scared of taking adventures. Also, the text states "Simon and his friends were scared to even go near it (the lighthouse)." This tells us that he is cowardly since he's scared to go near the lighthouse.

PSSA Practice Book, English Language Arts, Grade 5

13 In the first two paragraphs below, the author gives details about the lighthouse. Complete the table by listing **three** examples of factual details and **three** examples of Simon's personal opinions or feelings.

Simon was fascinated with the lighthouse to the south of the island. It was just two miles from his front door. The lighthouse stood proudly above the sea and cast its light for miles. It had stood in that spot for over two hundred years. Wind and rain had battered it, but the lighthouse stood strong and sturdy. During the day, you could see the aging of the old stone bricks.

Simon often stared at the lighthouse and wondered about its history. He had even heard rumors that it was haunted by a stonemason that had helped build it. He had been told the stonemason's initials were carved into some of the stones. Simon had never been close enough to see it for himself. At night it was an eerie presence. The white stones shone in the moonlight like a ghost hovering over the sea. Simon knew the lighthouse was meant to protect sailors. But sometimes he felt like it was watching him. Simon and his friends were scared to even go near it.

Factual Details	Simon's Opinions or Feelings
The lighthouse had been the for over 200 years.	Simon was scared to go near it.
The lighthouse was in the south of the island.	He felt it was watching him.
Its (job) is to protect sailors	He felt at night it was an eerie presence. Wind and rain. 2.

END OF PRACTICE SET

PSSA English Language Arts

Practice Set 2

Reading

Literary Text

Instructions

This set has one passage for you to read. The passage is followed by questions.

Read each question carefully. For each multiple-choice question, fill in the circle for the correct answer. For other types of questions, follow the instructions given. Some of the questions require a written answer. Write your answer on the lines provided.

Tara's Fear

Tara was scared of flying. She always had been ever since she was a little girl. It hadn't been a problem for her as a child though, as her parents never took a vacation overseas. Despite this, Tara's fear grew steadily the older she got. She hated the idea of being up in the air and in flight.

One year her family announced that they would take their vacation abroad. They were going to New Zealand. Her father had planned an adventure trip that included white water rafting, fly fishing, and trekking up an old volcano. Tara had just turned 13 years old. Everything her father described sounded like the kind of great adventure she had only read about in books. She was excited by the thought of it all, but she couldn't stop thinking about the long flight there. She longed to go, but she didn't know if she could cope with the flight there. She was so distraught that she finally claimed that she simply could not go. As she lay crying on her bed at the thought, her father walked into her room.

"I can't do it, Dad," she said sobbing. "I won't be able to fly."

Her father placed his hand gently on her shoulder.

"I know honey," he whispered. "It's really difficult for you. I know exactly how you feel."

Tara looked up at her father. "Do you really?" she asked.

"When I was your age, I had a phobia too," he replied. "I never thought I'd ever get over it."

Tara sat upright on the bed. She would never have guessed that her father could be scared of anything.

"What were you scared of Dad?" she asked.

Her father looked at her before replying.

"It seems silly now, but I used to be scared of spiders. Whenever I saw one I would scream and run in the other direction. When I was young, I didn't even like playing outside because of spiders and small insects. One year my mother told me that we were going camping. I immediately refused to go. The idea of sleeping under the stars with all of those bugs scared the life out of me!"

"What happened then, Dad?" asked Tara.

"Well my mother talked to me," he replied. "She explained that she understood why I was scared, but that it was something that she could help me to overcome. Then she told me that once I did get over my fear, I would be able to enjoy being outdoors much more. She made me realize that I couldn't let a spider stop me from ever enjoying being outdoors. I had to focus on all the fun I would be having, not on the one thing that scared me."

A small smile crept across Tara's face.

"So did you go in the end then, Dad?" she asked.

"You bet I did," he replied without hesitation. "It was a challenge, but I kept thinking about my mother's words. They inspired me to face my fears. I went camping with my family and had the time of my life. You'll have the time of your life on our trip. You can't let your fear of the plane stop you from having all those good times. You just close your eyes and imagine yourself in New Zealand and don't let your fear take the good times away from you."

Tara suddenly felt determined. She was going to stand up to her fear and not let it steal her trip from her.

"Thanks Dad," said Tara. "You'd better make sure you book me a seat on the plane because I'm coming whether my fear likes it or not."

1. What does the word <u>distraught</u> mean in the sentence below?

   She was so distraught that she finally claimed that she simply could not go.

   Ⓐ Disbelieving
   ● Ⓑ Distressed
   Ⓒ Uncertain
   Ⓓ Determined

2. In the sentence below, which word means about the same as <u>steadily</u>?

   Despite this, Tara's fear grew steadily the older she got.

   Ⓐ Swiftly
   Ⓑ Weirdly
   Ⓒ Suddenly
   ● Ⓓ Gradually

3. How does Tara feel when her father first says that he had a phobia?

   ● Ⓐ Alarmed
   Ⓑ Surprised
   Ⓒ Excited
   Ⓓ Relieved

4. Based on the information in paragraph 2, explain why Tara has mixed feelings about the trip to New Zealand. Use details from the passage to explain your answer.

Tara had mixed feelings about going to New Zealand of excitment and fear. She was excited to have a fun adventure, but had a phobia of flying on an airoplane.

5. Read this sentence spoken by the father.

   The idea of sleeping under the stars with all of those bugs scared the life out of me!

   Which literary device does the father use to emphasize how fearful he felt?

   Ⓐ Imagery, using details to create an image or picture

   Ⓑ Hyperbole, using exaggeration to make a point

   Ⓒ Simile, comparing two items using the words "like" or "as"

   Ⓓ Symbolism, using an object to stand for something else

6. Which statement best describes how you can tell that the passage is realistic fiction?

   Ⓐ It has a theme that can be applied in real life.

   Ⓑ It describes events that could really happen.

   Ⓒ It has a modern setting.

   Ⓓ It has a main problem.

7. How do the father's past experiences help him know how to help his daughter? Use details from the passage to support your answer.

   The fathers experiences help him know how to help because he understands what having a phobia feels like.

8. How are Tara and Tara's father similar?

   Ⓐ They have the same fear of flying.

   Ⓑ They have never flown before.

   Ⓒ They receive help to overcome a fear from a parent.

   Ⓓ They are thoughtful and understanding.

9 The main theme of the passage is about –

- Ⓐ admitting your fears
- Ⓑ letting other people help you
- ● not letting your fears hold you back
- Ⓓ making the most of every opportunity

10 Complete the cause and effect diagram below to show how Tara and Tara's father are affected by their fears.

Cause | Effect

Tara's Fear	What It Prevents Her Doing
Fear of flying on airoplane	traveling

Tara's Father's Fear	What It Prevents Him Doing
arachnaphobia (fear of spiders)	going outside/ camping

11 At the end of the passage, Tara says that she is going on the plane whether her fear likes it or not. Explain what Tara means by this.

Tara meant that she wasn't going to let her fear control what she was going to do.

12 In the passage, Tara wants to do the things her father has planned for them in New Zealand. Explain how this helps her be braver.

This makes Tara braver because ~~she is~~ even though she is scared of going on an airoplane, she still plans to do it.

END OF PRACTICE SET

PSSA English Language Arts

Practice Set 3

Reading

Informational Text

Instructions

This set has one passage for you to read. The passage is followed by questions.

Read each question carefully. For each multiple-choice question, fill in the circle for the correct answer. For other types of questions, follow the instructions given. Some of the questions require a written answer. Write your answer on the lines provided.

Mark Zuckerberg

Mark Zuckerberg is a web site developer and computer programmer. He is also a businessperson. He is best known for creating the web site Facebook. Facebook is a web site that allows people to connect with friends and family. He is now the CEO and president of the company.

Zuckerberg founded the web site in 2004 with some of his Harvard University classmates. He has since overseen the development of the site. Facebook became the most visited online web site throughout 2010. This was also the year that Mark Zuckerberg was named as Person of the Year by *Time Magazine*.

Mark Zuckerberg was born in White Plains, New York in 1984. His early education was spent at Ardsley High School. This was followed by Phillips Exeter Academy. While at Phillips Exeter Academy, he won prizes for his work in science, mathematics, astronomy, and physics. His outdoor pursuits included fencing, and he was captain of the college fencing team. He is also multilingual and can speak French, Latin, Hebrew, and Ancient Greek.

Zuckerberg first showed an interest in computers during middle school. At this time, he started to write software programs. His father hired an experienced software developer, David Newman, to tutor his son. He was identified at this young age to be an amazing talent. This encouraged him to take a graduate course in software design while at high school. He continued to develop computer programs as he learned.

Zuckerberg's main interest was in software that helped people to interact and communicate. This passion inspired a program called ZuckNet. This allowed a small set of users to communicate by 'pinging' each other. It was like a basic version of today's instant messenger tools. Zuckerberg continued to experiment with different software programs. Then he enrolled at Harvard University. During this time, he focused on creating software that connected people through common interests. The inspiration for Facebook came from paper-based books at the university. The books were known as facebooks and showed students' names, photographs, and gave information about them.

Facebook was launched on February 4, 2004. At first it was only for Harvard University students. It soon spread to other major universities including Stanford, Columbia, Yale, and MIT. This was followed by a spread to most universities in the United States. In 2005, it was made available to high schools. This was followed by allowing people from large companies like Apple and Microsoft to join. In 2006, it was made available to anyone over the age of 13. The site has grown rapidly since then. In 2012, Facebook had over one billion users worldwide.

On May 18, 2012, Facebook took another major step in its history. It listed on the stock exchange. It was one of the biggest listings in history. On the day of its listing, Facebook had a total value of just over $100 billion. Mark Zuckerberg was given the honor of ringing the bell to open stock market trading on the day. He rang the bell from the Facebook campus in California surrounded by cheering staff.

The site continues to grow and change. As of January 2014, Zuckerberg remains as chairman and CEO of Facebook, and has an estimated total wealth of just over $25 billion. In 2010, he pledged to give at least half of his wealth to charity over his lifetime. His donations have included giving over $100 million to public schools in New Jersey, supporting various small Internet businesses, and giving almost $1 billion worth of Facebook shares to the Silicon Valley Community Foundation.

One other thing Mark Zuckerberg is known for is wearing hoodies. While a suit and tie is the expected choice for a business meeting, he appears at many wearing a hoodie and slide-on sandals. This kind of casual clothing is also usually his choice for presentations and other public events. Some have said that his style of dress shows his lack of seriousness. Others argue that he values what he does above what he looks like.

© Elaine Chan and Priscilla Chan, Wikimedia Commons

1. As it is used in the sentence, what does the word <u>common</u> mean?

   During this time, he focused on creating software that connected people through common interests.

   Ⓐ   Ordinary

   Ⓑ   Everyday

   ●   Shared

   Ⓓ   General

2. Read this sentence from the passage.

   He is also multilingual and can speak French, Latin, Hebrew, and Ancient Greek.

   What does the prefix in the word <u>multilingual</u> mean? Explain how the sentence helps show the meaning of the prefix.

   I think it means you can speak multiple languages. The sentence helps show the meaning because it says he can speak French, Latin, Hebrew, and Greek which are multiple languages.

3 Place the following groups in order from first to gain access to Facebook to last to gain access to Facebook. Write the numbers 1, 2, 3, and 4 on the lines to show the order.

__2__ Students of major universities

__3__ Employees of large companies

__4__ High school students

__1__ Harvard University students

4 Which paragraph has the main purpose of describing how Zuckerberg first developed his computer skills? Circle the paragraph you have selected.

Paragraph 1   Paragraph 2   Paragraph 3   Paragraph 4

Paragraph 5   Paragraph 6   Paragraph 7   Paragraph 8

5 Which sentence from the passage best shows that Facebook is successful?

- (Ⓐ) *Facebook is a web site that allows people to connect with friends and family.*
- Ⓑ *Facebook became the most visited online web site throughout 2010.*
- Ⓒ *Facebook was launched on February 4, 2004.*
- Ⓓ *This was followed by allowing people from large companies like Apple and Microsoft to join.*

6 Why did Mark Zuckerberg's father most likely hire a software developer to tutor his son?

- Ⓐ He was worried that Mark was making mistakes.
- **Ⓑ** He saw that Mark had a talent worth developing.
- Ⓒ He saw that Mark was struggling with his studies.
- Ⓓ He wanted Mark to develop useful programs.

7 This passage is most like –

- **Ⓐ** a biography
- Ⓑ an autobiography
- Ⓒ a short story
- Ⓓ a news article

8 In paragraph 3, the author describes how Zuckerberg won prizes for his work in several areas, was captain of the fencing team, and is multilingual. Explain why you think the author chose to include these details.

I think that the author chose to include these details because they were cools facts about Mark Zuckerberg. Paragraph 3 was also stating facts about him so they stated this too.

27

9 The web below summarizes information from the passage.

```
            What Mark
            Zuckerberg is
            Best Known As
         /       |        \
  business-   web site    computer
   person     developer   programmer
```

Complete the web by choosing the **two** best options from those given below. Write your answers in the web.

| teacher | fencing champion | computer programmer |
| web site developer | author | college professor |

10 The passage describes how successful Mark Zuckerberg has become. Describe **one** lesson about becoming successful people can learn from the passage. Use details from the passage in your answer.

I think people can learn that it is a process and you need to be patient. This is because it took a while for Facebook to become available to everyone and be famous, as it shows in the text.

11 What does the photograph and the caption show about Zuckerberg's personality? Explain your answer.

I think it shows that he is pretty chill. I think this because he doesn't care about looking proper and fancy, and instead would rather be comfortable. He is chill about what he wears.

END OF PRACTICE SET

PSSA English Language Arts

Practice Set 4

Reading

Informational Text

Instructions

This set has one passage for you to read. The passage is followed by questions.

Read each question carefully. For each multiple-choice question, fill in the circle for the correct answer. For other types of questions, follow the instructions given. Some of the questions require a written answer. Write your answer on the lines provided.

Sir Isaac Newton

Sir Isaac Newton was an English-born physicist and mathematician. He also had a keen interest in astronomy, philosophy, alchemy, and theology. He was born on January 4, 1643 and died on March 31, 1727 at the age of 84. It was in the field of physics where Sir Isaac Newton carried out his best and most important work.

Newton is widely recognized as the first person to understand gravity. He also developed the three laws of motion. These laws became the foundations for scientists' work through the following centuries. Newton's work showed that the motion of objects is governed by a rigid set of natural laws. These laws applied to objects on the earth as well as the planets themselves.

Sir Isaac Newton's thirst for knowledge was applied to all aspects of science. He studied the speed of sound, and designed the first reflecting telescope for practical use. He also developed an advanced theory of color. He even developed a universal law of cooling.

Newton's Laws of Motion

Newton's First Law of Motion	An object will remain at rest unless acted on by an unbalanced force.
Newton's Second Law of Motion	The acceleration of an object depends on its mass and the net force.
Newton's Third Law of Motion	For every action, there is an equal and opposite reaction.

Sir Isaac Newton's work in the field of mathematics was also groundbreaking. His studies are said to have advanced every mathematics theory in practice today. Credit for some of his findings is shared with a German philosopher called Gottfried Leibniz. The basis of their work was applied to developing fractions and equations as mathematical tools. His continued hard work in the field led to him being appointed a Professor of Mathematics in 1669.

Sir Isaac Newton was also a deeply religious man. It is a little known fact that he wrote more papers on religion than he did on physics and mathematics. Many of his religious papers were ahead of their time. They were opposed to many beliefs held in the 17th century.

Sir Isaac Newton is widely considered to be one of the most influential men of all time. His work has inspired much of the scientific and mathematical knowledge that is widely used today. Despite this, Newton was a modest man who often praised the work of others who had gone before him. In 1999, a poll of modern experts revealed that Sir Isaac Newton was considered to be the greatest physicist of all time. He shared the title with Albert Einstein.

1 Read this sentence from the passage.

> **Despite this, Newton was a modest man who often praised the work of others who had gone before him.**

As it is used in the sentence, what does the word <u>modest</u> mean?

- Ⓐ Humble
- Ⓑ Kind
- Ⓒ Simple
- Ⓓ Shy

2 Read this sentence from the passage.

> **Sir Isaac Newton's thirst for knowledge was applied to all aspects of science.**

What does the phrase "thirst for knowledge" refer to?

- Ⓐ The intelligence to understand difficult subjects
- Ⓑ A commitment to helping others learn
- Ⓒ The ability to absorb and remember information
- Ⓓ A desire to know everything

3 According to the passage, in which area did Sir Isaac Newton carry out his most important work?

- Ⓐ Mathematics
- Ⓑ Physics
- Ⓒ Theology
- Ⓓ Astronomy

4 How would this passage be different if it were an autobiography?

    Ⓐ   It would be a more factual summary of Newton's theories.

    Ⓑ   It would include references to prove the statements made.

    Ⓒ   It would include quotes from other sources.

    Ⓓ   It would be written by Isaac Newton himself.

5 Which paragraph has the main purpose of describing Sir Isaac Newton's contributions to physics? Circle the paragraph you have selected.

    Paragraph 1   **(Paragraph 2)**   Paragraph 3

    Paragraph 4   Paragraph 5   Paragraph 6

6 What is the main purpose of the information in the table? In your answer, explain how the information in the table relates to the rest of the passage.

I think the main purpose of the paragraph was to explain what Isaac Newton did in physics. This relates to the rest of the passage since It's about Isaac Newton and facts about him/what he did.

7 Give **two** details the author includes to support the idea that Sir Isaac Newton had a strong influence on science.

Supporting Detail 1:

He developed the three laws of motions and was the first person to understand gravity.

Supporting Detail 2:

He designed the first reflecting telescope for practical use.

8 Complete the table below by listing **two** other fields of study and summarizing Newton's major achievements in the field.

Field of Study	Major Achievements
Physics	He developed the three laws of motions and was the first person to understand gravity.
Mathematics	His studies are said to have advanced every mathematics theory in practice today.
Science	He designed the first reflecting telescope.

9 How does the author show that Sir Isaac Newton had a strong influence on science? Use details from the passage to support your answer.

The author shows that Sir Isaac Newton had a strong influence on science. The text states, "...Sir Isaac Newton was considered to be the greatest physcist of all time." This shows that he was one of the best which tells us that he did a lot! The text also states," Newton is widely recognized as the first person to understand gravity." This proves that he helped by figuring out gravity. As you can see, he had a big influence on science.

END OF PRACTICE SET

PSSA English Language Arts

Practice Set 5

Reading and Writing

Literary Text with Writing Task

Instructions
This set has one passage for you to read. The passage is followed by questions. Read each question carefully. For each multiple-choice question, fill in the circle for the correct answer. For other types of questions, follow the instructions given. Some of the questions require a written answer. Write your answer on the lines provided.

Spinning the Spider's Web

The spider spins his silken web,
In the corner of my home,
He weaves it for his family,
One teeny space their own.

I watch him as he toils,
Through the hours of the day,
Spinning as the summer burns,
Forever building come what may.

And when his web is broken,
He never sheds a tear,
He simply spins and starts again,
And keeps his loved ones near.

This small kingdom is his castle,
And a tiny place to rest,
Although some may beg to differ,
He builds his home to be the best.

He goes about his business,
And does not seek to pry or scare,
He means no harm to those around him,
To cross your path, he wouldn't dare.

The spider just keeps on spinning,
His winding, silken web,
Building homes amongst the darkness,
Keeping family in good stead.

So next time you see the spider,
Spinning webs inside your home,
Think how hard he has to toil,
Without a single word or moan.

PSSA Practice Book, English Language Arts, Grade 5

1. Read this line from the poem.

   I watch him as he toils,

   What does the word <u>toils</u> mean?
   - (A) Works ✓
   - (B) Spins
   - (C) Struggles
   - (D) Plays

2. Read this line from the poem.

   One teeny space their own.

   Complete the chart by dividing the words listed below into synonyms of <u>teeny</u> and antonyms of <u>teeny</u>.

   ~~tiny~~   <u>giant</u>   ~~small~~   massive

   <u>little</u>   ~~huge~~   great   ~~minute~~

Synonyms	Antonyms
tiny	giant
little	huge
small	great
minute	massive

3 What does the poet seem to find most impressive about spiders?

    Ⓐ   That they can live anywhere

    Ⓑ   That they never stop working

    Ⓒ   That they are not afraid of anything

    Ⓓ   That they leave people alone

4 Think about your answer to Question 3. Write **two** lines below that support your answer to Question 3. Explain what each line shows about the poet's opinion of spiders.

Line 1: "I watch him as he toils through the hours of the day"

Line 2: "Thinks how hard he has to toil, without a single word or moan"

5 Which stanza of the poem has a message about facing disappointments?

    Ⓐ   Stanza 1

    Ⓑ   Stanza 2

    Ⓒ   Stanza 3

    Ⓓ   Stanza 4

6 Based on your answer to Question 5, explain how the poet communicates the message about overcoming disappointments.

The poet communicates the message about overcoming dissapointments in stanza three. In the text it states "When his web is broken, he never sheds a tear, he simply starts spinning again..." This shows the author was telling us that when the spider is dissapointed, he doesn't get upset and instead just moves on and keep going.

7 Which literary technique does the poet use in the first line of the poem?

- Ⓐ Alliteration
- Ⓑ Simile
- **Ⓒ Metaphor** (selected)
- Ⓓ Flashback

8 What is the rhyme pattern of each stanza of the poem?

- Ⓐ All the lines rhyme with each other.
- Ⓑ There are two pairs of rhyming lines.
- **Ⓒ The second and fourth lines rhyme.** (selected)
- Ⓓ None of the lines rhyme.

9 Which statement would the poet most likely agree with?

- Ⓐ People should make their own homes like spiders do.
- Ⓑ People should keep their homes free from spider webs.
- Ⓒ People should be aware of the dangers of spiders.
- **Ⓓ** People should leave spiders alone.

10 The poet states that "to cross your path, he wouldn't dare." What does the phrase "cross your path" refer to?

- **Ⓐ** Scaring someone
- Ⓑ Running into someone
- Ⓒ Stealing from someone
- Ⓓ Arguing with someone

11 Describe what people can learn from the spider about hard work and determination.

Lessons people can learn from the spider from the spider is to work hard and keep going and even when its hard, don't give up.

12 Select the line from the poem that contains a metaphor.

☐ *I watch him as he toils,*

☐ *Through the hours of the day,*

☐ *He simply spins and starts again,*

☑ *This small kingdom is his castle,*

☐ *He builds his home to be the best.*

☐ *His winding, silken web,*

☐ *So next time you see the spider,*

☐ *Think how hard he has to toil,*

13 Describe the meaning of the metaphor identified in Question 12. In your answer, explain what the metaphor shows about the spider's home.

It shows that his small web is more than that like how a "small kingdom" is actually a "castle."

14 Imagine what it is like to be the spider. Write a story from the point of view of the spider describing **one** of the events below in the spider's life.

- when the web breaks and he has to start again
- when he finally finishes spinning the web
- when he sees a person worrying about him and his web

In your story, tell what the spider does and how the spider feels.

Most of my day is spent perfecting my web. I spin and spin until it is done. I am spinning right now. I am almost done spinning, when my web suddenly brakes! This doesn't happen all the time but today is one of those times. It can be dissapointing to see something I've worked so hard on breaks but I've learnt there's no point pouting so I just start again. After more hard work, I finnally finish. It looked pretty good. Right then, I see a pair of big blue eyes across from me. Fear spreads around my body and I stay as still as can be. It can be scary coming across a human. Two things can happen in this situation; they could either scream or run away, or they can swat at me or call someone else to do it. I've been lucky so far, but what if... Thankfully right then, the human just walked away and I realized he didn't see me after all. I was relieved as I went back to my busy day as a spider.

END OF PRACTICE SET

PSSA English Language Arts

Practice Set 6

Reading and Writing

Literary Text with Writing Task

Instructions

This set has one passage for you to read. The passage is followed by questions.

Read each question carefully. For each multiple-choice question, fill in the circle for the correct answer. For other types of questions, follow the instructions given. Some of the questions require a written answer. Write your answer on the lines provided.

The Bees, the Wasps, and the Hornet

A store of honey had been found in a hollow tree. The wasps stated that it belonged to them. The bees were just as sure that the treasure was theirs. The argument grew very heated. It looked as if the affair could not be settled. But at last, with much good sense, they agreed to let a judge decide the matter. They brought the case before Judge Hornet.

When Judge Hornet called the case, witnesses stated that they had seen certain winged creatures in the neighborhood of the hollow tree. The creatures had hummed loudly, had striped bodies, and were yellow and black.

The wasps stated that this described them. The bees stated that this described them.

This did not help Judge Hornet make a decision. He said he wanted to take a few days to think about the case. When the case came up again, both sides had a large number of witnesses.

Judge Hornet sighed. He knew it was going to be a long day. Then the eldest bee asked if he could address the court.

"I'll allow it," Judge Hornet said.

"Your honor," the eldest bee said, "the case has now been going on for a week. If it is not decided soon, the honey will not be fit for anything. I move that the bees and the wasps be both instructed to make some honey. Then we shall soon see to whom the honey really belongs."

The wasps began to panic. They jumped up and down and complained loudly. Wise Judge Hornet quickly understood why they did so.

"It is clear," said Judge Hornet, "who made the honey and who could not have made it. The honey belongs to the bees."

1 Read this sentence from the passage.

The argument grew very heated.

The word <u>heated</u> suggests that the bees and wasps became –

    Ⓐ   confused

    Ⓑ   angry

    Ⓒ   warm

    Ⓓ   tired

2 In the sentence below, why does the author use the word <u>treasure</u>?

The bees were just as sure that the treasure was theirs.

    Ⓐ   To suggest that the honey was gold

    Ⓑ   To show that the honey was hidden

    Ⓒ   To show that the honey had been there a long time

    Ⓓ   To suggest that the honey was precious

3 What is the main purpose of the first paragraph?

    Ⓐ   To describe the main problem

    Ⓑ   To compare the bees and the wasps

    Ⓒ   To introduce the setting

    Ⓓ   To describe how to solve an argument

4 The main lesson the wasps learn is about being —

- Ⓐ hardworking
- Ⓑ honest
- Ⓒ prepared
- Ⓓ skilled

5 Based on your answer to Question 4, explain how the outcome for the wasps shows the main lesson.

_____

_____

_____

_____

_____

6 How is the passage mainly organized?

- Ⓐ Two events are compared and contrasted.
- Ⓑ Events are described in the order they occur.
- Ⓒ Facts are given to support an argument.
- Ⓓ A question is asked and then answered.

7 Why do the wasps most likely panic when the elder bee suggests that the judge should instruct the bees and wasps to make honey?

Ⓐ The wasps know they cannot make honey.

Ⓑ The wasps are too tired to make honey.

Ⓒ The wasps think the bees' honey will taste better.

Ⓓ The wasps think it will take too long.

8 Explain what the judge decides when he sees the wasps panicking. Explain how the wasps' actions cause the judge to reach his decision.

_____

_____

_____

_____

_____

9 Based on his suggestion, the eldest bee is best described as —

Ⓐ impatient

Ⓑ polite

Ⓒ wise

Ⓓ cranky

10 The passage states that "when the case came up again, both sides had a large number of witnesses." How does this influence the events?

- Ⓐ It makes the wasps sorry for their actions because they realize how much the bees care about the honey.
- Ⓑ It makes the wasps upset and nervous because they fear being embarrassed in front of so many people.
- Ⓒ It makes the judge want to be sure to make the right decision because he knows how important it must be to both sides.
- Ⓓ It makes the judge open to listening to the ideas of the eldest bee because the judge wants to find a faster solution.

11 Complete the table below by describing **one** way the bees and the wasps are similar and **one** way the bees and the wasps are different. In the second column, describe how the similarity or difference affects the events of the passage.

Similarity	Effect on the Events
Difference	**Effect on the Events**

12 How can you tell that the events in the passage could not really happen? Use details from the passage in your answer.

_____

_____

_____

_____

_____

13 What is the main problem in the passage? How is the main problem solved? Use details from the passage to support your answer.

_____

_____

_____

_____

_____

14 In the passage, the wasps learn that it does not pay to lie. Think about a time when you lied to get something you wanted. Write a story that tells about that time. In your story, describe why you lied and what happened after you lied.

END OF PRACTICE SET

PSSA English Language Arts

Practice Set 7

Language

Writing and Editing Tasks

Instructions

The first four questions in this set are writing tasks. Read the information and then answer the questions.

This set also has short passages that contain errors or opportunities for improvement. Read each passage and answer the questions that follow it. For each multiple-choice question, fill in the circle for the correct answer. For other types of questions, follow the instructions given.

A student is writing a research paper about different uses of kites. Read the source below. Then answer the following two questions.

> Kite-flying is another worldwide sport. It was popular with old and young in China at the time when the Egyptians were cutting stones for the pyramids. Benjamin Franklin learned the nature of lightning using a kite. He used the old bow kite, the kind that every beginner learns to make.
>
> The hexagonal kite is more reliable, and is quite as cheap and as easily made. Kites of both these kinds have been used to get a line from a stranded vessel to the shore, and engineers have used them. They did it when the first suspension bridge was built at Niagara, to get a line across the chasm, which gradually grew into the great suspending cables. Kites have been used to draw light vehicles over smooth ground, and they make good sport when made to draw sleds over the ice.

1 Circle **two** sentences from the source that could be used to show that kites have had important uses other than being just toys.

2 Write a short paragraph that tells how kites are more than just toys. Use details from the sentences you circled in your paragraph.

_____

_____

_____

_____

_____

The following is part of an opinion letter a student is writing for the school newspaper. Read the paragraph. Then answer the following two questions.

> The book-reading challenge last month was held to raise money. I think it was a great idea. Every student was asked to try to read as many books as possible, and our teacher suggested we try to read at least one a week. The problem is that there just wasn't enough time. We already have homework and lots of students have sports training as well. It was too much to try to fit in and it wasn't enjoyable. It is still a great idea, but I think it should be held during school vacation next time. Reading should be fun and shouldn't be stressful like that.

3 Write a few sentences that could be used to start the paragraph. The sentences should state the main idea of the paragraph.

_____

_____

_____

4 The student wants to add more reasons to support the idea that the challenge shouldn't be held during school weeks. List **two** more reasons the student could include in the letter.

1. _____

_____

2. _____

_____

The passage below contains errors. The words or phrases that are incorrect are underlined. For each word or phrase underlined, answer the question below.

Australia

Australia is not only a country, <u>and</u> it is also a continent. In 1851, gold was discovered in Australia. This discovery <u>leaded</u> to many people traveling <u>their</u> from all over the world. By 1859, there were six colonies. In 1901, they <u>agree</u> to form a commonwealth.

Australia now has eight states and territories. New South Wales is the state with the largest <u>poppulation</u>. It also has the largest city, <u>that</u> is Sydney. The capital of Australia is Canberra. It is in the Australian Capital Territory.

5 Which of these should replace <u>and</u>?
- Ⓐ but
- Ⓑ if
- Ⓒ or
- Ⓓ so

6 Which of these should replace <u>leaded</u>?
- Ⓐ led
- Ⓑ leads
- Ⓒ leading
- Ⓓ lead

7 As it is used in the sentence, what is the correct spelling of <u>their</u>? Write your answer below.

_____

8 Which of these should replace <u>agree</u>?
- Ⓐ agrees
- Ⓑ agreed
- Ⓒ agreeing
- Ⓓ agreeable

9 What is the correct way to spell <u>poppulation</u>? Write your answer below.

_____

10 Which of these should replace <u>that</u>?
- Ⓐ who
- Ⓑ which
- Ⓒ where
- Ⓓ which

The passage below contains errors. The words or phrases that are incorrect are underlined. For each word or phrase underlined, answer the question below.

Comets

Comets are balls of dust or ice that move <u>threw</u> the atmosphere. They come from two <u>diffrent</u> places in space. One is known as the Kuiper Belt. <u>The other place Oort Cloud.</u>

Both of those locations are orbiting the Sun. But they are far from the Sun. The Kuiper Belt is just past Neptune. The Oort Cloud is <u>very</u> farther away. It is far out past even Pluto.

They are so far away that the ice making up the comets does not melt. However, sometimes comets do come closer to the Sun. Then the ice <u>began</u> to melt. This leaves a trail behind them. This gives comets their unique <u>appearence</u>.

11   Which of these should replace <u>threw</u>?
- Ⓐ   thru
- Ⓑ   though
- Ⓒ   through
- Ⓓ   thought

12   What is the correct way to spell <u>diffrent</u>? Write your answer below.

_____

13. Which of these is the correct way to write a complete sentence?
    Ⓐ The other place is Oort Cloud.
    Ⓑ The other place the Oort Cloud.
    Ⓒ The other place named Oort Cloud.
    Ⓓ The other place is the Oort Cloud.

14. Which of these should replace <u>very</u>?
    Ⓐ most
    Ⓑ much
    Ⓒ more
    Ⓓ many

15. Which of these should replace <u>began</u>?
    Ⓐ begin
    Ⓑ begins
    Ⓒ beginning
    Ⓓ begun

16. Which of these should replace <u>appearence</u>?
    Ⓐ appearince
    Ⓑ appearance
    Ⓒ appearinse
    Ⓓ appearanse

The passage below contains errors. The words or phrases that are incorrect are underlined. For each word or phrase underlined, answer the question below.

Rookie

Today was my first day of basketball practice. We had to <u>where</u> shirts that have numbers and our names on the back. One of the first things I learned is that bouncing the ball is called dribbling. When the coach first <u>tell</u> us, I <u>couldnt</u> stop laughing about it! The coach said I should take basketball more <u>serious</u>.

Most of the lesson was spent trying to throw the ball up and into the hoop. At first, the balls <u>was</u> going everywhere. It was as if the basketballs had minds of their own. I got better at it and I scored three baskets! I am excited for when I will be good enough to play <u>me</u> first game.

17 Which of these should replace <u>where</u>?

- Ⓐ were
- Ⓑ wear
- Ⓒ we're
- Ⓓ ware

18 Which of these should replace <u>tell</u>?

- Ⓐ tells
- Ⓑ told
- Ⓒ telling
- Ⓓ tolded

19 Write the word <u>couldnt</u> by adding the apostrophe in the correct place. Write your answer below.

_____

20 Which of these should replace <u>serious</u>?
- Ⓐ seriously
- Ⓑ seriouser
- Ⓒ seriousness
- Ⓓ seriousest

21 Which of these should replace <u>was</u>?
- Ⓐ be
- Ⓑ is
- Ⓒ are
- Ⓓ were

22 Which of these should replace <u>me</u>?
- Ⓐ mine
- Ⓑ its
- Ⓒ their
- Ⓓ my

END OF PRACTICE SET

PSSA English Language Arts

Practice Set 8

Writing

Opinion Piece Writing Task

Instructions

This set contains a writing task. Read the writing prompt. Use the planning page to plan your answer. Then write your answer on the blank lines.

Opinion Piece Writing Prompt

Do you think students should be allowed to have cell phones at school? Why or why not?

Write an opinion piece that tells whether or not students should be allowed to have cell phones at school. Give at least three reasons to support your opinion.

Planning Space
You can take notes and plan your work in the space below. Then write your opinion piece on the lined pages.

END OF PRACTICE SET

PSSA English Language Arts

Practice Set 9

Reading and Writing

Informational Text with Writing Task

Instructions

This set has one passage for you to read. The passage is followed by questions.

Read each question carefully. For each multiple-choice question, fill in the circle for the correct answer. For other types of questions, follow the instructions given. Some of the questions require a written answer. Write your answer on the lines provided.

Playing a Musical Instrument

Playing a musical instrument is a popular pastime for all age ranges. Young or old, it is lots of fun to play a musical instrument. There are many different types to choose from including guitar, flute, piano, trumpet, and saxophone.

Making a Choice

First, you need to choose a musical instrument that you would like to learn how to play. Here are some things you should think about:

- the cost of the instrument
- how easy or difficult the instrument is to learn
- whether there is a teacher available to help you learn it
- what opportunities there will be to play it

You might also think about the kind of music you'd like to play. This will probably be the kind of music that you also enjoy listening to.

Another thing to consider is whether you'd like to play music alone or as part of a group. If you want to play alone, you might like to play the piano. This would not be a great choice if you'd like to play in a marching band! A trumpet or a trombone would be a better choice for that. If you'd like to play in a small group, you might choose the violin or the cello. String instruments like these are often played together in groups of two to four musicians. If you're imagining playing in a rock band, the guitar or the drums are popular choices. If you imagine yourself playing in a huge orchestra, you have lots of choices. You could play anything from the flute, to the saxophone, to the piano or the drums.

One other thing to consider is whether you would also like to sing as well. Some instruments are great for this, while others are not so good. It would be nearly impossible to sing while playing the trumpet! If you want to sing as well, consider learning the piano or the guitar. Just remember that you will have to work hard on your singing skills as well as your playing skills.

Getting Your Gear

Now you have chosen your instrument, you need to buy it. If it is expensive, you might like to borrow it instead. You might know a friend or relative who plays an instrument. You can ask to borrow an instrument for a little while to try it out. That way, you can make sure it is the right choice before spending lots of money. Some schools or libraries will lend students instruments. Or you can look in your local paper or online for a secondhand instrument.

Getting Ready to Learn

After you have your instrument, you should then create a learning plan. This might involve private lessons with a music teacher or going to music classes. Some people choose to learn on their own. You can use books, movies, web sites, or you can even watch videos online.

To learn quickly, your plan may include a variety of learning methods. Make sure that you attend every lesson or study your books regularly. Also, be sure to practice what you have learned as this is the best way to develop your new skill.

Making Music

Once you have learned enough to play a song, you should start playing for people. Many people get nervous when they first start performing. You might find that you make more mistakes than usual. Don't let this get you down. Remember that you will learn to calm and control your nerves the more you practice. It is often a good idea to start with your family or friends. Or you might play for your music class. Once you become confident, you can then play for larger groups of people.

Keep Going

To become a good musician, you have to keep playing. Keep learning as much as you can and practice often. Challenge yourself to learn more difficult songs as well. As you learn more, you will become better and better. Some people even become good enough to play music as a career.

1. Read this sentence from the passage.

   Playing a musical instrument is a popular pastime for all age ranges.

   What does the word <u>pastime</u> mean?

   Ⓐ　Choice

   Ⓑ　Career

   Ⓒ　Sport

   Ⓓ　Hobby

2. According to the passage, what should you do first?

   Ⓐ　Check to see if your school will lend you an instrument

   Ⓑ　Decide what instrument you would like to play

   Ⓒ　Create a plan for learning to play an instrument

   Ⓓ　Look in your local newspaper for an instrument

3. Under which heading is information provided about deciding what type of instrument to learn to play? Circle the correct answer.

   Making a Choice   Getting Your Gear

   Getting Ready to Learn   Making Music   Keep Going

4 Read this sentence from the passage.

Keep learning as much as you can and practice often.

Which word means the opposite of <u>often</u>?

- Ⓐ Never
- Ⓑ Rarely
- Ⓒ More
- Ⓓ Regularly

5 The author provides the most information in the section "Making a Choice." Explain why you think this is such an important step. Give at least **two** reasons in your answer.

_____

_____

_____

_____

_____

6 The web below lists ways that people can learn to play a musical instrument on their own.

```
[Read books]                    [           ]
           \                   /
            [Ways to Learn on
                Your Own]
           /                   \
[Watch movies]                  [           ]
```

Which of these best complete the web? Write your answers in the web.

Watch videos online	Find a tutor
Attend a class	Visit web sites

7 What is the main purpose of the passage?

　Ⓐ　To give readers guidance and advice

　Ⓑ　To entertain readers with a story

　Ⓒ　To teach people how to play a musical instrument

　Ⓓ　To compare different musical instruments

8 Read this sentence from the section "Making Music."

It is a good idea to start with your family or friends.

Why does the author most likely suggest starting with your family or friends?

- Ⓐ So your friends will want to learn to play as well
- Ⓑ So your family will see that you are trying hard
- Ⓒ So you feel more comfortable playing
- Ⓓ So you can have people join in

9 Which sentence from "Making Music" best supports your answer to Question 8?

- Ⓐ *Many people get nervous when they first start performing.*
- Ⓑ *You might find that you make more mistakes than usual.*
- Ⓒ *Remember that you will learn to calm and control your nerves the more you practice.*
- Ⓓ *Or you might play for your music class.*

10 Why does the author use bullet points in the passage?

- Ⓐ To highlight the main points
- Ⓑ To list a set of ideas
- Ⓒ To show steps to follow in order
- Ⓓ To describe items that are needed

11 Complete the web below by listing **three** ways you could save money when getting a musical instrument.

```
        ┌─────────────────────┐
        │   Saving Money on   │
        │   Your Instrument   │
        └─────────────────────┘
       /           |           \
 ┌─────────┐  ┌─────────┐  ┌─────────┐
 │         │  │         │  │         │
 │         │  │         │  │         │
 └─────────┘  └─────────┘  └─────────┘
```

12 The photograph of the girl at the end of the passage is probably included to suggest which of the following?

Ⓐ How much time and effort it takes to become good at playing

Ⓑ How it is best to choose an instrument you can play on your own

Ⓒ How enjoyable and rewarding playing an instrument is

Ⓓ How it can be difficult to play for an audience at first

13 Complete the graphic organizer below by listing **two** instruments that would be suitable for each purpose.

- Playing in an orchestra
  - ☐
  - ☐

- Playing in a marching band
  - ☐
  - ☐

- Playing and singing
  - ☐
  - ☐

- Playing in a rock band
  - ☐
  - ☐

14 If you had to choose a musical instrument to learn to play, which type would you choose? Explain what you considered when making your choice. Use details from the passage in your answer.

In your response, be sure to
- describe which instrument you would choose
- explain why you made that decision
- explain what you considered to make your choice
- use details from the passage

END OF PRACTICE SET

PSSA English Language Arts

Practice Set 10

Reading and Writing

Literary Text with Writing Task

Instructions

This set has one passage for you to read. The passage is followed by questions.

Read each question carefully. For each multiple-choice question, fill in the circle for the correct answer. For other types of questions, follow the instructions given. Some of the questions require a written answer. Write your answer on the lines provided.

Trying Too Hard

Robert was determined to do well in his exams. He devoted all of his spare time to study. He had always wanted to be a lawyer when he grew up. He wanted to go to a good college and enjoy a successful career. Unfortunately, this meant that he was almost always serious. Even though he was young, he was unable to relax and enjoy himself most of the time. His friends often got frustrated that he didn't want to spend much time with them.

Robert had an important exam the following day. He had spent almost an entire week preparing for it. He had managed to get little sleep and was very tired.

He even spent the night before the exam revising and had barely managed any sleep at all. However, he thought that he was ready for the exam. He was confident that he had worked harder than anyone else and was sure to get a perfect grade.

After Robert ate his breakfast, he started to feel a little ill. He was tired and unable to focus. He also had a small headache and found it very difficult to concentrate. He still refused to believe that he could ever fail the exam. Robert arrived at the school hall and took his seat beside his friends. He noticed how relaxed and happy they looked compared to him.

"They are just underprepared," he thought to himself as he began the exam.

Despite his best efforts, Robert struggled. The numbers seemed to swim in front of him. After twenty minutes, he felt very hot and uncomfortable. He then slumped in his chair, and one of his friends called for help. The school doctor suggested that he was exhausted and would be unable to complete the exam.

He spent the lunch break in the nurse's office. He looked out the window and watched his friends. They smiled and joked and seemed to have not a care in the world. Robert decided that from then on, he wouldn't take it quite so seriously. He would study enough, but never too much.

1   What does the word <u>frustrated</u> mean in the sentence below?

   His friends often got frustrated that he didn't want to spend much time with them.

   Ⓐ   Worried

   Ⓑ   Annoyed

   Ⓒ   Confused

   Ⓓ   Amused

2   What does the word <u>underprepared</u> mean in the sentence below?

   "They are just underprepared," he thought to himself as he began the exam.

   Ⓐ   The most prepared

   Ⓑ   More prepared

   Ⓒ   Not prepared enough

   Ⓓ   Too prepared

3   Think about the genre of "Trying Too Hard." What is the main feature the passage shares with a fable?

   Ⓐ   It features mythical creatures.

   Ⓑ   It involves forces of nature.

   Ⓒ   It has a moral lesson.

   Ⓓ   It is set in the past.

4 Describe **two** important details about Robert's character that are introduced in the first paragraph.

1: _____

_____

2: _____

_____

5 Complete the diagram by listing **four** details the author includes to show that Robert is not well on the day of the exam.

Robert is unwell on the day of the exam.

6 Which sentence best explains why Robert feels ill during the exam?

- Ⓐ *Robert had an important exam the following day.*
- Ⓑ *He had spent almost an entire week preparing for it.*
- Ⓒ *He even spent the night before the exam revising and had barely managed any sleep at all.*
- Ⓓ *He was confident that he had worked harder than anyone else and was sure to get a perfect grade.*

7 What happens right after Robert slumps in his chair?

- Ⓐ He keeps working on the exam.
- Ⓑ The nurse comes to see him.
- Ⓒ He starts to feel sick.
- Ⓓ His friend calls for help.

8 How does the photograph in the passage suggest that Robert is studying too hard? Explain your answer.

_____

_____

_____

_____

_____

9 Complete the diagram below by describing what Robert expects to happen and what actually happens.

Cause   **Effect**

What Robert Does	→	What He Expects to Happen
Robert studies very hard for his exam.	→	What Actually Happens

10 Irony occurs when someone's actions have an effect that is the opposite of what was intended. Use your answer to Question 9 to explain why the outcome of the exam is ironic.

_____

_____

_____

_____

_____

11. Which of these describes the main lesson that Robert learns in the passage?

   Ⓐ   It is important to have a balanced life.

   Ⓑ   It is better to have fun than to do well.

   Ⓒ   You should never give up on your goals.

   Ⓓ   You can achieve anything if you believe in yourself.

12. Which sentence from the passage best summarizes the lesson you selected in Question 11?

   Ⓐ   *Robert was determined to do well in his exams.*

   Ⓑ   *He still refused to believe that he could ever fail the exam.*

   Ⓒ   *They smiled and joked and seemed to have not a care in the world.*

   Ⓓ   *He would study enough, but never too much.*

13. How would the ending of the passage most likely be different if it was told from Robert's point of view?

   Ⓐ   The reader would have a better understanding of Robert's feelings about what happened.

   Ⓑ   The reader would realize that Robert is probably not really going to change.

   Ⓒ   The reader would worry more about whether or not Robert will be allowed to retake the exam.

   Ⓓ   The reader would not feel sorry for Robert since what happened was his own fault.

14 At the end of the passage, Robert decides that he shouldn't take things too seriously. Why does Robert make this decision? Do you think this is a good decision? Explain why or why not.

In your response, be sure to
- describe why Robert decides not to take things too seriously
- explain whether or not you think Robert makes a good decision
- explain why you feel that way
- use details from the passage to support your answer

END OF PRACTICE SET

PSSA English Language Arts

Practice Set 11

Reading and Writing

Informational Text with Writing Task

Instructions

This set has one passage for you to read. The passage is followed by questions.

Read each question carefully. For each multiple-choice question, fill in the circle for the correct answer. For other types of questions, follow the instructions given. Some of the questions require a written answer. Write your answer on the lines provided.

The Super Bowl

The Super Bowl is the deciding game of the National Football League (NFL). It decides who wins the championship trophy each season. It was first played in the winter of 1967 to find the champion of the 1966 season. Since that time, it has become a major national occasion loved by football fans everywhere. It is a major honor to win the Super Bowl for both teams and their supporters.

At the time it was created, there were two American football leagues. These were the NFL and the AFL, or American Football League. The winners of each league would play against each other to determine which team was the overall champion.

When the two leagues merged, the game was retained. It has since become a game where the top national teams play each other for the main championship. The Green Bay Packers won the first two Super Bowls played in 1967 and 1968. They were considered to be the best team at the time. Many people thought they would continue to win for years to come. This changed in 1969 when the New York Jets won Super Bowl III. This was the last Super Bowl that included teams from separate NFL and AFL leagues.

The game has grown steadily in popularity since this time. It is played annually on a Sunday. The timing of the game has changed since 1970. While it used to be played in early January, it is now played on the first Sunday in February. The Super Bowl game has become a major part of America's culture. It has even been declared a national holiday across the nation.

The Super Bowl has emerged as the most watched television event in America. Super Bowl XLV was played in 2011 and drew a national audience of more than 110 million viewers. The Super Bowl is also one of the most watched sporting events throughout the world. Only the UEFA Champions League trophy in soccer is viewed by a higher global audience.

The Pittsburgh Steelers have won a total of six Super Bowls. They stand alone as the most successful team in the contest's history. The Dallas Cowboys and the San Francisco 49ers have each won the trophy five times. The Pittsburgh Steelers had a chance to win a seventh title in the 2011 Super Bowl. However, they were defeated by the Green Bay Packers. It was the fourth win for the Green Bay Packers.

Sports and Trophies

Trophies are an important part of major sporting leagues. They become a symbol of what every team hopes to achieve and act as a lasting symbol of the winning team's achievements. They often have a long history that makes them even more special.

The Vince Lombardi Trophy

The team that wins the Super Bowl receives the Vince Lombardi Trophy. It is named after the coach of the Green Bay Packers who won the first two Super Bowl games. It was designed by the vice president of Tiffany & Co. in 1966 and the trophies have been made by the company ever since.

It was first presented to the Green Bay Packers in 1967, though it was simply known as the championship trophy at that time. Its name was changed in 1970 after Vince Lombardi passed away. Unlike some other trophies, a new Vince Lombardi trophy is made each year and the winning team keeps that trophy forever.

The Larry O'Brien Championship Trophy

The Larry O'Brien Championship Trophy is awarded to the winning team of the National Basketball Association (NBA) finals each year. The name of the winning team and the year is engraved on the trophy, and given to the winning team to keep. The trophy is named after Larry O'Brien, who was the NBA commissioner from 1975 to 1984.

The trophy is made by Tiffany & Co. each year. It is made from silver alloys and coated in 24 karat gold. The golden color of the trophy is striking and distinguishes it from other trophies. However, despite its striking appearance, it is not as well known as many other sporting trophies.

The Stanley Cup

The Stanley Cup is the most appreciated ice hockey trophy in the world. It is awarded every year to the winner of the National Hockey League (NHL) championships.

Unlike most other sports, a new Stanley Cup is not made each year. Instead, the winning team keeps the trophy until new champions are crowned the next year. This ability to take possession of the trophy for a short time makes players appreciate the award even more. Each winning team also has the names of players, coaches, and other team staff engraved on the trophy. This is considered a great honor by all.

The Stanley Cup is the oldest professional sports trophy in North America. It was donated by the Governor General of Canada, Lord Stanley of Preston, in 1892.

1 Read this sentence from the passage.

When the two leagues merged, the game was retained.

Which word means about the same as <u>retained</u>?

- Ⓐ Changed
- Ⓑ Kept
- Ⓒ Improved
- Ⓓ Removed

2 According to the passage, how has the Super Bowl changed since it was introduced?

- Ⓐ It is watched by less people.
- Ⓑ It is played between more teams.
- Ⓒ It is played in a different month.
- Ⓓ It is held on a Saturday.

3 How is the third paragraph mainly organized?

- Ⓐ A problem is described and then a solution is given.
- Ⓑ Events are described in the order they occurred.
- Ⓒ Two teams are compared and contrasted.
- Ⓓ Facts are given to support an argument.

4 Determine whether each sentence in paragraph 1 is a fact or an opinion. Write F or O on each line to show your choice.

___ The Super Bowl is the deciding game of the National Football League (NFL).

___ It decides who wins the championship trophy each season.

___ It was first played in the winter of 1967 to find the champion of the 1966 season.

___ Since that time, it has become a major national occasion loved by football fans everywhere.

___ It is a major honor to win the Super Bowl for both teams and their supporters.

5 According to the passage, which team has won the most Super Bowls?

Ⓐ Green Bay Packers

Ⓑ Pittsburgh Steelers

Ⓒ Dallas Cowboys

Ⓓ New York Jets

6 Which inference can best be made based on the information in the passage?

Ⓐ Vince Lombardi was a respected coach.

Ⓑ Vince Lombardi was replaced after the Green Bay Packers were defeated in 1969.

Ⓒ Vince Lombardi still coaches the Green Bay Packers today.

Ⓓ Vince Lombardi was a football player before he became a coach.

7 Which meaning of the word <u>drew</u> is used in the sentence below?

> **Super Bowl XLV was played in 2011 and drew a national audience of more than 110 million viewers.**

- Ⓐ Attracted
- Ⓑ Sketched
- Ⓒ Dragged
- Ⓓ Tied

8 Which statement made in paragraph 1 is best supported by the paragraph below? Explain your answer.

> **The Super Bowl has emerged as the most watched television event in America. Super Bowl XLV was played in 2011 and drew a national audience of more than 110 million viewers. The Super Bowl is also one of the most watched sporting events throughout the world. Only the UEFA Champions League trophy in soccer is viewed by a higher global audience.**

_____

_____

_____

_____

_____

_____

9 Choose **two** sentences from the paragraph below that support the idea that the Super Bowl is a major occasion in the United States. Circle the **two** sentences below.

> The game has grown steadily in popularity since this time. It is played annually on a Sunday. The timing of the game has changed since 1970. While it used to be played in early January, it is now played on the first Sunday in February. The Super Bowl game has become a major part of America's culture. It has even been declared a national holiday across the nation.

10 Based on your answer to Question 9, explain why you chose the two sentences.

_____

_____

_____

_____

_____

11 In the sentence below, which word could best be used in place of <u>appreciate</u>?

> **This ability to take possession of the trophy for a short time makes players appreciate the award even more.**

Ⓐ Notice

Ⓑ Demand

Ⓒ Ignore

Ⓓ Value

12 What makes the Stanley Cup special? In your answer, explain how it differs from the Vince Lombardi Trophy and the Larry O'Brien Championship Trophy.

_____

_____

_____

_____

_____

_____

13. How does the last paragraph of "The Stanley Cup" help show the importance of the trophy?

   Ⓐ It shows that ice hockey has been played for a long time.

   Ⓑ It shows that ice hockey is a national sport.

   Ⓒ It shows the long history of the trophy.

   Ⓓ It shows that the trophy is most important to Canadians.

14. Describe **two** facts given about the Larry O'Brien Championship Trophy.

   1: _____

   _____

   2: _____

   _____

15. Describe **two** opinions given about the Larry O'Brien Championship Trophy.

   1: _____

   _____

   2: _____

   _____

16 Write an essay that describes how the history of sports can play a major role in making them special today. In your answer, give at least **two** examples of how history adds to the meaning of a sport.

In your response, be sure to
- describe how the history of sports helps make them special today
- give at least **two** examples of how history adds to the meaning of a sport
- use details from the passage to support your answer

_____

_____

_____

_____

_____

_____

_____

_____

_____

_____

_____

END OF PRACTICE SET

PSSA English Language Arts

Practice Set 12

Reading and Writing

Informational Text with Writing Task

Instructions

This set has one passage for you to read. The passage is followed by questions.

Read each question carefully. For each multiple-choice question, fill in the circle for the correct answer. For other types of questions, follow the instructions given. Some of the questions require a written answer. Write your answer on the lines provided.

To My Teacher

June 15, 2013

Dear Miss Hooper,

I am writing to thank you for the help you have given me this year. We have covered many subjects in class and you have helped me with every single one. You explain things so clearly, and are also amazingly patient. I really believe you have a great skill for teaching others. Without your assistance, I would of struggled to do as well as I have. You should be very proud of the way that you help children to learn. It is because of you that I am thinking about becoming a teacher when I am older.

There were so many highlights this year. Whatever the subject, you made it fun and interesting to everyone. All of your students found learning new things so easy because of you. You never once made me feel silly for asking a question. You were always willing to explain something again and again until I understood.

I have mixed feelings about school next year. Firstly, I guess I am sad that you will no longer be my teacher. However, I am pleased that other children will get to share your knowledge. It would be selfish for me to keep you to myself all through school! I hope that they thank you for the good work that you do. You deserve it and it is the least we can do.

I did not enjoy school much before this year. I was new to the school this year. At my old school, I found learning difficult and quite a challenge. It made me so nervous about starting a new school, but the change turned out to be a huge blessing. The last nine months have changed everything. I am now very confident and looking forward to the next school year.

Thank you once again. You have truly been a great teacher and helped me greatly. I hope that we may even share the same classroom again one day.

Yours sincerely,

Jacob Maclean

1 Read this sentence from the letter.

There were so many highlights this year.

What does the word <u>highlights</u> refer to?

- Ⓐ The best parts
- Ⓑ Challenges
- Ⓒ Breakthroughs
- Ⓓ Main ideas

2 Circle the **two** words from the passage that have about the same meaning.

help	pleased	interesting	selfish
fun	difficult	assistance	proud

3 Which sentence from the passage is a fact?

- Ⓐ *Whatever the subject, you made it fun and interesting to everyone.*
- Ⓑ *I really believe you have a great skill for teaching others.*
- Ⓒ *You should be very proud of the way that you help children to learn.*
- Ⓓ *I was new to the school this year.*

4. What is the main reason Jacob wrote the letter?

   Ⓐ   To tell how he wants to become a teacher

   Ⓑ   To explain that he is leaving the teacher's class

   Ⓒ   To express his thanks to his teacher

   Ⓓ   To encourage his teacher to keep working hard

5. Which sentence best summarizes the main idea of the letter?

   Ⓐ   *It is because of you that I am thinking about becoming a teacher when I am older.*

   Ⓑ   *I have mixed feelings about school next year.*

   Ⓒ   *I did not enjoy school much before this year.*

   Ⓓ   *You have truly been a great teacher and helped me greatly.*

6. Jacob describes Miss Hooper as "amazingly patient." Describe **two** details given in the passage that show her patience.

   1: _____

   _____

   2: _____

   _____

7 How does Jacob feel about not having Miss Hooper as his teacher next year?

- Ⓐ Upset and angry
- Ⓑ Pleased and excited
- Ⓒ Sad, but understanding
- Ⓓ Confused, but unconcerned

8 Based on your answer to Question 7, explain how you can tell that Jacob feels this way.

_____

_____

_____

_____

_____

9 Which detail best explains why Jacob appreciates Miss Hooper so much?

- Ⓐ After this year, Jacob will not be taught by Miss Hooper.
- Ⓑ Before Miss Hooper, Jacob always found learning difficult.
- Ⓒ During the year, Jacob struggled more than all the other students.
- Ⓓ At his last school, Jacob was bored and made little effort.

10 Select **all** the statements that are effects Miss Hooper had on Jacob.

☐ Making him look forward to school next year

☐ Making him want to become a teacher

☐ Making him want to join more school clubs

☐ Helping him learn more

☐ Helping him make new friends

☐ Helping him become more confident

11 Jacob states that starting a new school "turned out to be a huge blessing." Explain why Jacob feels this way.

_____

_____

_____

_____

_____

12 Look at the chart below.

Why Jacob Thinks Miss Hooper is a Good Teacher

1) She is patient.
2)
3)

Complete the chart by writing **two** of the sentences below in the empty spaces.

She is funny.	She is well-trained.	She explains things clearly.
She is proud.	She makes class fun.	She gives challenging work.

13 Read this paragraph from the passage.

> **Thank you once again. You have truly been a great teacher and helped me greatly. I hope that we may even share the same classroom again one day.**

How does this paragraph relate to the ideas of the rest of the passage?

Ⓐ It introduces new ideas.

Ⓑ It presents evidence against the main ideas.

Ⓒ It restates the main ideas.

Ⓓ It gives details to support the main ideas.

14 Think about how Jacob describes Miss Hooper. Choose the **one** quality Miss Hooper has that you think is most important for a good teacher. Explain why you chose that quality and why it is most important. You can use information from the passage and your own ideas and experiences to support your answer.

In your response, be sure to
- identify the **one** quality Miss Hooper has that you think is most important
- explain how you can tell that Miss Hooper has that quality
- explain why you feel that quality is most important

END OF PRACTICE SET

PSSA English Language Arts

Practice Set 13

Reading and Writing

Literary Text with Writing Task

Instructions

This set has one passage for you to read. The passage is followed by questions.

Read each question carefully. For each multiple-choice question, fill in the circle for the correct answer. For other types of questions, follow the instructions given. Some of the questions require a written answer. Write your answer on the lines provided.

Little White Lily
By George Macdonald

1. Little White Lily
   Sat by a stone,
   Drooping and waiting
   Till the sun shone.

2. Little White Lily
   Sunshine has fed;
   Little White Lily
   Is lifting her head.

3. Little White Lily
   Said: "It is good
   Little White Lily's
   Clothing and food."

4. Little White Lily
   Dressed like a bride!
   Shining with whiteness,
   And crowned beside!

5. Little White Lily
   Drooping with pain,
   Waiting and waiting
   For the wet rain.

6. Little White Lily
   Holdeth her cup;
   Rain is fast falling
   And filling it up.

7. Little White Lily
   Said: "Good again,
   When I am thirsty
   To have the nice rain.

8. Now I am stronger,
   Now I am cool;
   Heat cannot burn me,
   My veins are so full."

9. Little White Lily
   Smells very sweet;
   On her head sunshine,
   Rain at her feet.

10. Thanks to the sunshine,
    Thanks to the rain,
    Little White Lily
    Is happy again.

1. Read these lines from the poem.

   Little White Lily
   Is happy again.

   Which literary device does the poet use in these lines?

   Ⓐ Simile

   Ⓑ Metaphor

   Ⓒ Personification

   Ⓓ Hyperbole

2. Based on your answer to Question 1, explain how the literary device helps readers connect with the poem.

   _____

   _____

   _____

   _____

   _____

3 Based on the poem, what is most important to the lily?

- Ⓐ Having water
- Ⓑ Smelling nice
- Ⓒ Being appreciated
- Ⓓ Getting shelter

4 What is the rhyme pattern of each stanza of the poem?

- Ⓐ The second and fourth lines rhyme.
- Ⓑ There are two pairs of rhyming lines.
- Ⓒ The first and last lines rhyme.
- Ⓓ None of the lines rhyme.

5 Select **all** the lines below that contain alliteration.

- ☐ *Sat by a stone,*
- ☐ *Drooping and waiting*
- ☐ *Sunshine has fed;*
- ☐ *Shining with whiteness,*
- ☐ *Rain is fast falling*
- ☐ *Heat cannot burn me,*
- ☐ *Thanks to the rain,*

6 Which of the following is used throughout the poem?

    Ⓐ   Symbolism, using an object to stand for something else

    Ⓑ   Hyperbole, using exaggeration to make a point

    Ⓒ   Repetition, repeating words, phrases, or lines

    Ⓓ   Flashback, referring back to an event in the past

7 Why does the poet compare the lily to a bride?

    Ⓐ   To show how special the lily feels

    Ⓑ   To emphasize how white the lily is

    Ⓒ   To explain that the lily is being used in a wedding

    Ⓓ   To suggest that the lily moves slowly

8 Read these lines from the poem.

> **Little White Lily**
> **Drooping with pain,**
> **Waiting and waiting**
> **For the wet rain.**

These lines suggest that the lily feels –

    Ⓐ   confident

    Ⓑ   desperate

    Ⓒ   calm

    Ⓓ   angry

9 In which stanza does the lily feel about the same as in the first stanza? Circle the stanza you have chosen.

    Stanza 2   Stanza 3   Stanza 4   Stanza 5   Stanza 6

    Stanza 7   Stanza 8   Stanza 9   Stanza 10

10 Think about how the lily feels in the first stanza and the stanza you identified in Question 9. Compare and contrast why the lily feels that way in each stanza.

_____

_____

_____

_____

_____

11 The poet probably uses the word <u>drooping</u> in the first paragraph to create a sense of —

    Ⓐ   determination

    Ⓑ   sadness

    Ⓒ   loneliness

    Ⓓ   relaxation

12 Read these lines from the poem.

> **Little White Lily**
> **Holdeth her cup;**
> **Rain is fast falling**
> **And filling it up.**

Explain what these lines are describing. Why can what is described not happen until the sun is shining?

_____

_____

_____

_____

_____

13 Complete the table below by listing **two** stanzas that include dialogue. For each stanza, describe what the dialogue tells the reader.

Stanza	What the Dialogue Tells the Reader

14 Explain how the weather affects the lily. In your answer, describe how the lily changes as the weather changes. Use details from the poem in your answer.

In your response, be sure to
- describe how the lily changes as the weather changes
- explain why the weather changes affect the lily
- use details from the poem in your answer

END OF PRACTICE SET

PSSA English Language Arts

Practice Set 14

Reading and Writing

Informational Text with Writing Task

Instructions

This set has one passage for you to read. The passage is followed by questions.

Read each question carefully. For each multiple-choice question, fill in the circle for the correct answer. For other types of questions, follow the instructions given. Some of the questions require a written answer. Write your answer on the lines provided.

Manchester United Soccer Club

About Soccer

1. Soccer is a ball sport that was invented in England in the 1800s. It is an outdoor sport. An individual match sees two teams of 11 players compete against each other. The object of the game is to work the ball into one of the two goals positioned at each end of the field.

2. It is a sport that is played all over the world. It is most popular in South America and Europe. The most successful international team is Brazil. They have won five World Cups since 1930, which is a competition that is held every 4 years. Italy has won four World Cups. Germany is not far behind, with three wins.

3. Soccer is not as popular as sports like baseball and football in the United States. The 2013 championship match of Major League Soccer in America had a crowd of 21,650. This is much less than for the Super Bowl, which had 71,000 people. However, soccer is a very entertaining sport to watch. Soccer may become a favorite sport in the United States one day.

4. As with popular American sports, major teams enjoy the massive support of their fans. Manchester United Soccer Club is based in the United Kingdom and is one of the most-loved teams. The love that fans have of the team is based on their long history, their success, and the talented and popular players that have been part of the team.

A Famous Soccer Club

5. Manchester United is a famous soccer team. They are based in the United Kingdom. They play in the English Premier League and the European Champions League. They are known as one of the most successful soccer clubs in the world.

6. They were first formed in 1888. At this time, they were named the Newton Heath Football Club. In 1901, they were sold and were given the new name of Manchester United.

7. They are the most successful club in the English League. They have won the English Premier League nineteen times. This is one more than their nearest rivals, Liverpool.

8. Since 1958, Manchester United have also won the European Champions League three times. This competition features teams from across Europe. It is this success that has helped them become such a well-known team.

9. David Beckham is one of the club's most famous players. He played for Manchester United from 1993 until 2003. In this time, he scored 62 goals for the club and helped his team win eight championships. He scored some amazing goals, including one from the halfway line that floated above the goalkeeper's head and curved into the net. The goal became so famous that it was voted by the British public as number 18 on a list of 100 greatest sporting moments. Beckham was known for being able to curve or bend the ball. It allowed him to score some amazing goals. These thrilled fans and helped draw huge crowds to games.

©Wikimedia Commons

10. In 2007, Beckham made an unexpected move. He joined America's Major League Soccer, and began playing for Los Angeles Galaxy. He was paid around $6.5 million per year. One of the most interesting things about the deal was that Beckham was not just paid by the Los Angeles Galaxy team. He was also paid by all the teams in America's Major League Soccer. The teams agreed to this because they hoped that having such a major star in their league would attract more people to the sport.

Manchester United's English Premier League Grand Final Wins

Year	Team Defeated
1908	Aston Villa
1911	Aston Villa
1952	Tottenham
1956	Blackpool
1957	Tottenham
1965	Leeds United
1967	Nottingham Forest
1993	Aston Villa
1994	Blackburn Rovers
1996	Newcastle United
1997	Newcastle United
1999	Arsenal
2000	Arsenal
2001	Arsenal
2003	Arsenal
2007	Chelsea
2008	Chelsea
2009	Chelsea
2011	Chelsea

1 Which meaning of the word <u>object</u> is used in the sentence below?

> **The object of the game is to work the ball into one of the two goals positioned at each end of the field.**

- Ⓐ A goal or aim
- Ⓑ A type of item
- Ⓒ To argue against
- Ⓓ To refuse to do something

2 Which detail from the passage is an opinion?
- Ⓐ Soccer was invented in the 1800s.
- Ⓑ Soccer is an outdoor sport.
- Ⓒ Soccer teams have 11 players each.
- Ⓓ Soccer is entertaining to watch.

3 Complete the table by adding information about the **three** most successful international teams. Order the teams from most to least successful.

Most Successful International Teams	Number of World Cup Wins Since 1930
1.	
2.	
3.	

4 Where was the game of soccer invented?

    Ⓐ   England

    Ⓑ   Brazil

    Ⓒ   Italy

    Ⓓ   Germany

5 Draw lines to match each sentence in paragraph 3 with the best description of the sentence. The first sentence has been matched for you.

Sentence	Description
Soccer is not as popular as sports like baseball and football in the United States.	a prediction
The 2013 championship match of Major League Soccer in America had a crowd of 21,650.	the main claim
This is much less than for the Super Bowl, which had 71,000 people.	an opinion
However, soccer is a very entertaining sport to watch.	a comparison
Soccer may become a favorite sport in the United States one day.	a fact given to support a claim

(The first sentence is matched to "the main claim.")

6 Circle the **two** words from the passage that have about the same meaning.

formed	rivals	success	competition
famous	teams	named	well-known

7 Which sentence is best supported by the information in the table at the end of the passage?

Ⓐ *They have won the English Premier League nineteen times.*

Ⓑ *This is one more than their nearest rivals, Liverpool.*

Ⓒ *Since 1958, Manchester United have also won the European Champions League three times.*

Ⓓ *This competition features teams from across Europe.*

8 Write F next to the sentences that are facts. Write O next to the sentences that are opinions.

___ They are based in the United Kingdom.

___ In 1901, they were sold and were given the new name of Manchester United.

___ Since 1958, Manchester United have also won the European Champions League three times.

___ It is this success that has helped them become such a well-known team.

9 List **two** facts the author includes to show that Manchester United have been a successful team.

1: _____

_____

2: _____

_____

10 Paragraph 10 describes how David Beckham was paid by all the teams in America's Major League Soccer. Which idea from "About Soccer" does this detail best support?

 Ⓐ Soccer is played all over the world.

 Ⓑ Soccer is not as popular in America as other sports.

 Ⓒ Soccer teams in Europe enjoy massive support from their fans.

 Ⓓ Soccer is played by teams of 11 players.

11 What is the main purpose of the seventh and eighth paragraphs?

 Ⓐ To describe how the team formed

 Ⓑ To describe the team's achievements

 Ⓒ To explain why the team is successful

 Ⓓ To show that the team has improved over time

12 Complete the chart below by writing the correct number in each empty box.

Team	Number of Times Defeated by Manchester United in the English Premier League Final
Aston Villa	
Arsenal	
Tottenham	

13 Read this dictionary entry for the word <u>deal</u>.

> **deal** *noun*
> 1. a business agreement 2. a bargain 3. the treatment given to somebody 4. the distribution of cards

Now read this sentence from the passage.

> **One of the most interesting things about the deal was that Beckham was not just paid by the Los Angeles Galaxy team.**

Which definition of the word <u>deal</u> is used in the sentence above?

Ⓐ Definition 1
Ⓑ Definition 2
Ⓒ Definition 3
Ⓓ Definition 4

14 The author states that the popularity of Manchester United is partly based on "the talented players that have been part of the team." How does the information given about David Beckham support this statement? Use information from the passage to support your answer.

In your response, be sure to
- describe David Beckham's influence on Manchester United and the team's popularity
- explain how Beckham's influence supports the idea that Manchester United is popular because of its talented players
- use details from the passage in your answer

END OF PRACTICE SET

PSSA English Language Arts

Practice Set 15

Language

Writing and Editing Tasks

Instructions

The first four questions in this set are writing tasks. Read the information and then answer the questions.

This set also has short passages that contain errors or opportunities for improvement. Read each passage and answer the questions that follow it. For each multiple-choice question, fill in the circle for the correct answer. For other types of questions, follow the instructions given.

A student is writing a research paper for history class about the first cars in America. The student found the paragraph below in the autobiography of Henry Ford. Read the paragraph. Then answer the following two questions.

> My "gasoline buggy" was the first and for a long time the only automobile in Detroit. It was considered to be something of a nuisance, for it made a racket and it scared horses. Also it blocked traffic. If I stopped my machine anywhere in town a crowd was around it before I could start up again. If I left it alone even for a minute some curious person always tried to run it. Finally, I had to carry a chain and chain it to a lamp post whenever I left it anywhere. And then there was trouble with the police. I do not know quite why, for my impression is that there were no speed-limit laws in those days. Anyway, I had to get a special permit from the mayor. I ran that machine about one thousand miles through 1895 and 1896 and then sold it to Charles Ainsley of Detroit for two hundred dollars. That was my first sale.

1 The student wants to write a paragraph about how people at the time were fascinated by cars. Circle **two** sentences from the source that could be used to support this idea.

2 The student wants to write a report about the problems cars caused at first. List **three** problems Ford had that the student could use in the report.

1. _____

2. _____

3. _____

A student is writing an article giving advice about being prepared for the school day. Read the plan for the article. Then answer the following two questions.

> Main idea: You will do better at school if you are well-prepared each day.
> Advice 1: Get up early each day so you do not feel rushed.
> Advice 2: Take the time to have a good breakfast.
> Advice 3: At the end of each day, check you have all your work done ready for the next day.

3 Write one or two sentences that could be used to start the article. The sentences should state the main idea of the article.

_____

_____

_____

4 Choose one of the pieces of advice listed. Write a paragraph giving that advice. In your paragraph, give **two** reasons the advice is important.

_____

_____

_____

_____

_____

_____

The passage below contains errors. The words or phrases that are incorrect are underlined. For each word or phrase underlined, answer the question below.

Dear Diary,

Today Mom and I go for a walk in the park after school. The park is such a pretty and peaceful place with all of the lovely trees flowers and birds. We saw people having picnics, and some kids rowing boats on the lake. Some people they were also feeding bread to the ducks.

We saw one man that was painted in silver paint. He was standing completely still and changing his pose every few minutes. While he was still, he looked exactly like a statue! It was pretty amazzing to watch. Mom and I took a photo in front of him. We said goodbye and left some chanje in his tip jar.

Harmanie

5   Which of these should replace go?
   Ⓐ   been
   Ⓑ   gone
   Ⓒ   going
   Ⓓ   went

6   Which of these punctuates lovely trees flowers and birds correctly?
   Ⓐ   lovely, trees flowers and birds
   Ⓑ   lovely, trees, flowers, and birds
   Ⓒ   lovely trees, flowers, and birds
   Ⓓ   lovely trees, flowers, and, birds

7 Which of these removes the correct word from the sentence below?

Some people they were also feeding bread to the ducks.

- Ⓐ Some people they also feeding bread to the ducks.
- Ⓑ Some people were also feeding bread to the ducks.
- Ⓒ Some they were also feeding bread to the ducks.
- Ⓓ Some people they were feeding bread to the ducks.

8 Which of these should replace that?
- Ⓐ which
- Ⓑ who
- Ⓒ whom
- Ⓓ whose

9 Which of these should replace amazzing?
- Ⓐ amazeing
- Ⓑ amazing
- Ⓒ ammazzing
- Ⓓ ammazzing

10 What is the correct way to spell chanje? Write your answer below.

_____

The passage below contains errors. The words or phrases that are incorrect are underlined. For each word or phrase underlined, answer the question below.

Dear Diary,

I've been trying for months now to solve the Rubik's Cube that Dad <u>buy</u> me last year. He knows that collecting odd and zany things is <u>the</u> fun hobby for me. That's one of the reasons I liked it so much. All you have to do to solve it is get the nine little squares on each side the same color. It sounds simple, <u>so</u> it is not! I've made a <u>pritty</u> pattern out of it, but haven't come close to solving it. <u>In fact it looks just as mixed up as when I first got it.</u> I will just have to try again tomorrow. No matter how long it takes, I am determined to solve it one day. When that day finally comes, I'll be <u>happy with myself</u> that I stuck with it.

Bye for now,

Terri

11 Which of these should replace <u>buy</u>?
- Ⓐ buyed
- Ⓑ buying
- Ⓒ bought
- Ⓓ boughted

12 Which of these should replace <u>the</u>?
- Ⓐ a
- Ⓑ an
- Ⓒ my
- Ⓓ that

13   Which of these should replace so?
   Ⓐ   and
   Ⓑ   but
   Ⓒ   or
   Ⓓ   nor

14   What is the correct way to spell pritty? Write your answer below.

   _____

15   Which of these places the comma in the correct place?
   Ⓐ   In fact, it looks just as mixed up as when I first got it.
   Ⓑ   In fact it, looks just as mixed up as when I first got it.
   Ⓒ   In fact it looks, just as mixed up as when I first got it.
   Ⓓ   In fact it looks just as mixed up as, when I first got it.

16   Which word would best replace the phrase happy with myself?
   Ⓐ   smiling
   Ⓑ   amazed
   Ⓒ   boasting
   Ⓓ   proud

The passage below contains errors. The words or phrases that are incorrect are underlined. For each word or phrase underlined, answer the question below.

Chess

Chess is a board game played on a checkerboard between two players. Each player has sixteen pieces. The goal <u>be</u> to use your pieces to trap or "checkmate" the king. A "checkmate" occurs when the king cannot move without being taken by <u>anuther</u> piece.

There are different rules for how each chess piece can move. <u>For example a rook can only move up or down.</u> A bishop can only move diagonally, and a knight can only move in an L-shape. The king can move in any direction, but can only move one space.

Chess is thought to have <u>develop</u> in India or China, and is one of the <u>most old</u> board games. During the 16th century, it became popular as a competitive board game. The game has continued to grow since then. The first World Chess Champion was Wilhelm Steinitz, <u>that</u> claimed the title in 1886.

17 Which of these should replace <u>be</u>?
- Ⓐ are
- Ⓑ been
- Ⓒ is
- Ⓓ was

18 What is the correct way to spell <u>anuther</u>? Write your answer below.

_____

19 Which of these places the comma in the correct place?

- Ⓐ For, example a rook can only move up or down.
- Ⓑ For example, a rook can only move up or down.
- Ⓒ For example a rook can only move, up or down.
- Ⓓ For example a rook can only move up, or down.

20 Which of these should replace develop?

- Ⓐ develops
- Ⓑ developed
- Ⓒ developing
- Ⓓ development

21 Which of these should replace most old?

- Ⓐ older
- Ⓑ oldest
- Ⓒ more older
- Ⓓ more oldest

22 Which of these should replace that?

- Ⓐ which
- Ⓑ who
- Ⓒ whom
- Ⓓ whose

END OF PRACTICE SET

PSSA English Language Arts

Practice Set 16

Writing

Informative/Explanatory Writing Task

Instructions

This set contains a writing task. Read the writing prompt. Use the planning page to plan your answer. Then write your answer on the blank lines.

Informative/Explanatory Writing Prompt

Think about the different holidays during the year and how they are celebrated. Choose the holiday that is most special to you. It could be the day you enjoy the most or the day that means the most to you.

Write an essay describing the holiday. Explain what you do on that day, how the holiday is celebrated, and why it is special to you.

Planning Space
You can take notes and plan your work in the space below. Then write your essay on the lined pages.

END OF PRACTICE SET

PSSA English Language Arts

Practice Set 17

Reading and Writing

Informational Texts with Writing Task

Instructions

This set has two short passages for you to read. Read each passage and answer the questions that follow it.

For each multiple-choice question, fill in the circle for the correct answer. For other types of questions, follow the instructions given. Some of the questions require a written answer. Write your answer on the lines provided.

After reading both passages, you will use information from both passages to answer a question. Write your answer on the lines provided.

Writing a Short Story
By Kevin Baker

Writing a short story is a popular and satisfying hobby for a lot of people. It is also an excellent way to express creative thoughts. Writing a good story is not easy, but it is certainly worth the effort. Here are the steps to take to write a good story.

Step 1

Every story starts with an idea. Start by thinking about the things that you enjoy. These activities are excellent subjects to base your stories on. Other ideas can come from thinking about subjects that you'd like to know more about.

Step 2

Once you have an idea, you can then decide who your main characters are going to be. Consider having both a hero and a villain in your story. This will help to keep your readers interested. A hero is also known as a protagonist, while a villain is known as an antagonist. You'll also need to think of the best location for your story to take place.

Step 3

Before you start writing, you need to plan your story. Most writers plan their stories by creating an outline. An outline is like an overview of the story. It should describe the main events that occur. Your story should have a beginning, a middle, and an end. This will help anyone who reads the story to follow its events.

Step 4

Now that you have your outline, it is time to start writing. Follow your outline and write your story. At this point, your story does not have to be perfect. You will go back and improve it later.

Step 5

The story you have written is your first draft. The next step is to read through it and revise it. Here are some questions to help you decide what might need to be changed:

- Are the events that happen clear?
- Is the story interesting?
- Have I described the characters well?
- Can I use better descriptions to make it more exciting?
- Have I left out any important points?
- Is the start of the story good enough to get the reader interested?
- Would the ending leave the reader feeling satisfied?

Keep working on your story until it is the best you can make it.

Step 6

Once the story is complete, read it in full to ensure that it is well-written and easy to follow. Make sure that all your sentences flow well and are easy to understand. You should also check for any spelling or grammar mistakes.

Step 7

It is now time to get some feedback on your story. Have others read your story so that they can make suggestions for improvements. Think about the advice that people tell you. You do not have to take all the advice given, but you should think about it.

Step 8

Revise your story again based on the feedback you have been given. You should also read through it again to make sure all your sentences are written correctly and to ensure that there are no spelling or grammar errors.

You should now have a well-written, polished, and entertaining story.

1. Read this sentence from the passage.

   You should now have a well-written, polished, and entertaining story.

   What does the word <u>polished</u> show about the story?

   Ⓐ It is enjoyable to read.

   Ⓑ It is smooth and free from errors.

   Ⓒ It has been well-planned.

   Ⓓ It has a suitable ending.

2. Based on your answer to Question 1, choose the **two** steps that will most ensure that the story is polished. Circle the steps you have chosen. Then explain why you chose those steps.

   Step 1   Step 2   Step 3   Step 4

   Step 5   Step 6   Step 7   Step 8

   _____

   _____

   _____

   _____

   _____

3 Read this sentence from the passage.

> **It is also an excellent way to express creative thoughts.**

Which meaning of the word <u>express</u> is used in the sentence?

- Ⓐ To send something quickly
- Ⓑ To put into words
- Ⓒ Plain or clear
- Ⓓ Direct or fast

4 Which detail about the author would best suggest that the advice in the passage can be trusted?

- Ⓐ He has kept a diary of his thoughts for many years.
- Ⓑ He has a college degree.
- Ⓒ His favorite hobby is reading.
- Ⓓ He has successfully published many short stories.

5 What is the main purpose of the passage?

- Ⓐ To teach readers how to do something
- Ⓑ To encourage people to read more
- Ⓒ To explain the purpose of writing
- Ⓓ To compare different types of hobbies

6 Why does the author use bullet points in the passage?

- Ⓐ To highlight the main points
- Ⓑ To list a set of ideas
- Ⓒ To show steps to follow in order
- Ⓓ To describe items that are needed

7 In which step is the first draft of the story written? Circle the correct step.

Step 1 Step 2 Step 3 Step 4

Step 5 Step 6 Step 7 Step 8

8 Explain what the terms <u>protagonist</u> and <u>antagonist</u> mean. Explain why you think having both in the story would help keep the reader interested.

_____

_____

_____

_____

_____

9 According to the passage, what should you do first when writing a story?

- Ⓐ Decide who the main character is going to be
- Ⓑ Write an outline of the story
- Ⓒ Discuss your story idea with other people
- Ⓓ Think of an idea for the story

10 The author states that "writing a good story is not easy." How does the information in the passage support this statement? Use details from the passage in your answer.

_____

_____

_____

_____

_____

The River Bank Creative Writing Group

Creative writing is a great way of expressing yourself. The problem is that many people never try to write. Many people believe that they do not have the ability. At the River Bank Creative Writing Group, we aim to unleash your creativity.

We are based in Brooklyn, New York. We started our community organization in the fall of 2001. In the years since then, we have brought creative writing into the lives of many local residents. It does not matter whether you wish to write creatively as a hobby or as a way of making money. We have experienced and skilled staff to help you achieve success. We start by teaching the very basics of creative writing. Then we develop a program that is unique to your skills and goals. This can focus on writing short stories, poetry, plays, or anything else that interests you.

So what exactly do we offer? Well, our creative workshops are known for their quality. Our teachers include experienced professional writers and editors. They will guide you and help you get started. They will also offer feedback on your writing to help you improve. We also have guest speakers who attend once a week and share their own advice and experience. These are usually published authors who have achieved success in their fields. Our guest list is varied and includes successful poets, short story writers, and novelists. Their practical experience is the key to unlocking your creative talents.

We have achieved some great results at the River Bank Creative Writing Group. In 2005, one of our earliest students had her first novel published. She has since gone on to enjoy two further publications and is known worldwide. In 2009, another of our writers had his first poetry collection published. Thousands of our other writers have emerged from our classes as skilled creative writers.

Our classes can benefit you regardless of your goals. If you wish to unlock your creative skill for an exciting pastime, then we can help you. If you dream of being a published author, then we can help you make that happen. It has never been easier to unlock your creativity. If you have an interest in creative writing, then contact us today. We are waiting to hear from you and ready to help you on your journey!

11 In the sentence below, what does the word <u>unleash</u> mean?

> **At the River Bank Creative Writing Group, we aim to unleash your creativity.**

- Ⓐ Take control of
- Ⓑ Train and shape
- Ⓒ Set free
- Ⓓ Benefit from

12 What is the main purpose of the fourth paragraph?
- Ⓐ To encourage people to take writing seriously
- Ⓑ To show the success of the writing group
- Ⓒ To describe different types of writing styles
- Ⓓ To suggest that getting published is easy

13 Describe **two** details given in the fourth paragraph that support your answer to Question 12.

1: _____

_____

2: _____

_____

14   What does the picture at the end of the passage most likely symbolize?

   Ⓐ   How long the writing group has existed for

   Ⓑ   How much of an achievement writing a book could be

   Ⓒ   How the teachers at the group are very experienced

   Ⓓ   How the writing group offers a range of services

15   From the information in the passage, the reader can conclude that the writing group –

   Ⓐ   is mainly for young writers

   Ⓑ   offers the services for free

   Ⓒ   is suited to all types of writers

   Ⓓ   considers publishing writers' works

16   The passage was probably written mainly to –

   Ⓐ   encourage people to attend the writing group's classes

   Ⓑ   highlight the benefits of creative writing

   Ⓒ   describe the history of the creative writing group

   Ⓓ   convince successful writers to be guest speakers

17 Complete the chart below by listing **three** ways the River Bank Creative Writing Group helps people develop their writing skills.

```
        ┌─────────────────┐
        │   Developing    │
        │  Writing Skills │
        └─────────────────┘
         /       |       \
   ┌─────┐  ┌─────────┐  ┌─────┐
   │     │  │         │  │     │
   │     │  │         │  │     │
   └─────┘  └─────────┘  └─────┘
```

18 Read these sentences from the passage.

> **If you wish to unlock your creative skill for an exciting pastime, then we can help you. If you dream of being a published author, then we can help you make that happen.**

Why does the author most likely include these sentences?

Ⓐ To warn the reader that the workshops may be difficult

Ⓑ To excite the reader about what may be possible

Ⓒ To suggest that the reader should have a clear goal

Ⓓ To describe the successes of past students

19 Which word best describes the tone of the passage?

- Ⓐ Comforting
- Ⓑ Straightforward
- Ⓒ Encouraging
- Ⓓ Modest

20 Select the **two** sentences from paragraph 2 that best support the idea that the River Bank Creative Writing Group tailors programs to suit each individual. Tick **two** boxes below to show your choices.

- ☐ *We are based in Brooklyn, New York.*
- ☐ *We started our community organization in the fall of 2001.*
- ☐ *In the years since then, we have brought creative writing into the lives of many local residents.*
- ☐ *It does not matter whether you wish to write creatively as a hobby or as a way of making money.*
- ☐ *We have experienced and skilled staff to help you achieve success.*
- ☐ *We start by teaching the very basics of creative writing.*
- ☐ *Then we develop a program that is unique to your skills and goals.*
- ☐ *This can focus on writing short stories, poetry, plays, or anything else that interests you.*

21 Describe how being a good writer involves getting other people to help you. In your answer, describe at least **two** ways other people can help you develop good writing skills. Use details from both passages in your answer.

In your response, be sure to
- describe how good writers need the help of others
- describe at least **two** ways other people can help you develop good writing skills
- use details from both passages to support your answer

END OF PRACTICE SET

PSSA English Language Arts

Practice Set 18

Reading and Writing

Literary Texts with Writing Tasks

Instructions

This set has two short passages for you to read. Read each passage and answer the questions that follow it.

For each multiple-choice question, fill in the circle for the correct answer. For other types of questions, follow the instructions given. Some of the questions require a written answer. Write your answer on the lines provided.

After reading both passages, you will use information from both passages to answer a question. Write your answer on the lines provided.

A New Start

August 2, 2013

Dear Aunt Jamie,

What a day! I started at my new school this morning and had the best time. I made lots of new friends and really liked my teachers. I was so nervous the night before, but I had no reason to be. Everyone was so friendly and polite. They made me feel at ease. It was like I'd been at the school for a hundred years!

The day started very early at exactly 7 o'clock. I didn't want to feel rushed, so I made sure to get up early. I had my breakfast downstairs with my mom. She could tell that I was very anxious. Mom kept asking me what was wrong. I admitted that I was scared that people wouldn't like me or that everyone would just ignore me. She told me I had nothing to worry about and that everyone was going to love me. If they didn't love me, Mom said to send them her way for a good talking to. I couldn't stop laughing.

My mom dropped me off at the school gates about ten minutes before the bell. A little blond girl got dropped off at the same time and started waving at me. She ran over and told me her name was Abigail. She was very nice and we became close straight away. We spent all morning together and began to chat to another girl called Stacey. The three of us sat together in class all day and we even made our way home together! It went so quickly. Our teacher told us that tomorrow we would really start learning and developing new skills.

It is late now so I am going to sleep, but I cannot wait until tomorrow! I feel as though I am really going to enjoy my time at my new school. I only hope that my new friends feel the same way too.

Lots of love,

Casey

1 Which of these is the opening of the letter?

    Ⓐ   *A New Start*

    Ⓑ   *August 2, 2013*

    Ⓒ   *Dear Aunt Jamie,*

    Ⓓ   *Lots of love,*

2 Read this statement from the first paragraph of the letter.

    What a day!

    Circle the emotion that best describes what Casey uses this statement to show. Then explain how the details in the first paragraph helped you choose your answer.

    nervousness   excitement   surprise   relief

    _____

    _____

    _____

    _____

3   Read this sentence from the letter.

She was very nice and we became close straight away.

What does Casey mean when she says that they "became close"?

Ⓐ   They began to be friends.

Ⓑ   They walked near each other.

Ⓒ   They stayed on their own.

Ⓓ   They were in the same class.

4   What will Casey most likely do when she arrives at school the next day?

Ⓐ   Sit by herself in the playground

Ⓑ   See if there are any other new people

Ⓒ   Look for Abigail and Stacey

Ⓓ   Go to class early to see her teacher

5   Which word means the opposite of polite?

Ⓐ   Rude

Ⓑ   Nice

Ⓒ   Easygoing

Ⓓ   Calm

6 The reader can tell that Casey's mother –

- Ⓐ is used to meeting new people
- Ⓑ is very worried about her daughter
- Ⓒ cares about Casey's feelings
- Ⓓ wishes Casey did not have to start a new school

7 Based on your answer to Question 6, describe how Casey's mother's actions show what she is like.

_____

_____

_____

_____

_____

8 Which word would Casey most likely use to describe Abigail?

- Ⓐ Funny
- Ⓑ Friendly
- Ⓒ Bossy
- Ⓓ Shy

9 Casey writes that "It was like I'd been at the school for a hundred years!" What is this an example of?

- Ⓐ Imagery, using details to create an image or picture
- Ⓑ Hyperbole, using exaggeration to make a point
- Ⓒ Flashback, describing events that occurred far in the past
- Ⓓ Symbolism, using an object to stand for something else

10 Think about your answer to Question 9. What is the statement Casey makes used to show?

- Ⓐ How bored Casey is
- Ⓑ How comfortable Casey feels
- Ⓒ How there is too much new information to take in
- Ⓓ How the school has a long history

11 How is Casey's day different from what she expected? Use details from the passage to support your answer.

_____

_____

_____

_____

_____

A New Arrival

Today was a very exciting day for me and my family. It was the day that my new baby brother came home from the hospital.

I remember when I first learned that I was going to have a new baby brother. "I have great news Emma," my mother said. "You are going to be a big sister." I just stared at my mother and I didn't even smile. I really wasn't sure what to think, but I had all these thoughts running through my head. I worried that he would drive me crazy by crying all the time. I worried that my parents might want him to have my room. I even worried that Mom would be too busy to come and watch me at my dance competitions.

All those things I worried about seem ridiculous now. I soon forgot about most of them anyway. By the time he was ready to arrive, I didn't have a single worry. I was far too excited about getting to meet him. I was looking forward to being his big sister and helping to look after him.

My baby brother was born yesterday morning at 9:51. My father came home in the afternoon and was overjoyed. He weighed 8 pounds and 1 ounce and my parents named him Bradley. My dad says that he is the most beautiful baby. I could barely sleep the night before. I was so excited about Bradley coming home. Eventually, I drifted off to sleep just as the morning sun began to rise.

I woke up as usual today at 9 o'clock. I went downstairs and enjoyed some toast for breakfast. I knew that my father was collecting my mother and Bradley at 11:30. I watched TV for a while before trying to read one of my favorite books. Whatever I tried to do, I just could not take my mind off my newborn brother. I couldn't help but try to imagine what he must look like. In my mind, he had bright blond hair and sparkling blue eyes. I wondered whether he would understand who I was when he first saw me. My daydreaming was interrupted by my dad's voice. "Let's go Emma," he called. It was finally time to leave.

I headed out to the car and we drove toward the hospital. I couldn't stop talking as we made our way through the winding roads. The short trip to the hospital seemed to take forever. We finally arrived at the hospital. We made our way through the reception and headed to the maternity ward. As we arrived at the doors, I could see my mother at the far end. She held a small bundle wrapped in a blue blanket in her arms.

Mom just smiled as I reached the end of her bed. She looked tired but extremely happy. I just stared for a few moments before Mom asked me if I wanted to meet my brother! I couldn't stop smiling and reached out in an instant. Mom held out her arms and passed Bradley to me.

I took him in my arms and cradled his tiny little baby body. As I looked down, he slowly opened his eyes and gazed up at me. They were the deepest blue that anyone could ever imagine. As I stroked his face he began to smile softly. Dad told me that he looks just like me when I was born. The thought that I was ever that beautiful made me smile. Then Bradley slowly closed his eyes and drifted off to sleep.

12 Which word best describes the tone of the sentence below?

I took him in my arms and cradled his tiny little baby body.

- Ⓐ Loving
- Ⓑ Casual
- Ⓒ Lively
- Ⓓ Serious

13 Which word means about the same as <u>overjoyed</u>?

My father came home in the afternoon and was overjoyed.

- Ⓐ Tired
- Ⓑ Delighted
- Ⓒ Relaxed
- Ⓓ Gloomy

14 Why does Emma most likely say that the trip to the hospital "seemed to take forever"?

- Ⓐ Her father got lost on the way.
- Ⓑ She was nervous about seeing her brother.
- Ⓒ She was excited and impatient.
- Ⓓ She lived far from the hospital.

15 Read this sentence from the passage.

> **They were the deepest blue that anyone could ever imagine.**

Which literary device is used in the sentence?

- Ⓐ   Alliteration, using words with the same consonant sounds
- Ⓑ   Hyperbole, using exaggeration to make a point
- Ⓒ   Simile, comparing two items using the words "like" or "as"
- Ⓓ   Symbolism, using an object to stand for something else

16 Which of these would Emma probably most look forward to doing the next day?

- Ⓐ   Reading her favorite book
- Ⓑ   Chatting with her father
- Ⓒ   Watching television
- Ⓓ   Rocking her brother to sleep

17 Which **two** words would Emma most likely use to describe her day? Tick the boxes of the words you have chosen.

- ☐ eerie
- ☐ surprising
- ☐ annoying
- ☐ disappointing
- ☐ special
- ☐ dull
- ☐ strange
- ☐ unforgettable

18 Which paragraph contains a flashback? Circle your choice. Then explain the purpose of the flashback.

| Paragraph 1 | Paragraph 2 | Paragraph 3 | Paragraph 4 |
| Paragraph 5 | Paragraph 6 | Paragraph 7 | Paragraph 8 |

_____

_____

_____

_____

19 How can you tell that the author is excited about having a baby brother? Use at least **two** details from the passage in your answer.

_____

_____

_____

_____

_____

20 Emma's first reaction to finding out she is going to have a brother can be described as selfish. List **two** details from the passage that show this.

1: _____

_____

2: _____

_____

21 Complete the web below by adding **three** more phrases from the paragraph below that create a sense of calm.

> I took him in my arms and cradled his tiny little baby body. As I looked down, he slowly opened his eyes and gazed up at me. They were the deepest blue that anyone could ever imagine. As I stroked his face he began to smile softly. Dad told me that he looks just like me when I was born. The thought that I was ever that beautiful made me smile. Then Bradley slowly closed his eyes and drifted off to sleep.

- stroked his face
- [ ]
- Phrases that Create a Sense of Calm
- [ ]
- [ ]

22 How do the experiences of Casey and Emma show that there is no need to be afraid of change? Use details from both passages in your answer.

In your response, be sure to
- describe what change Casey and Emma deal with and how things turn out
- explain how Casey's experience shows that change does not need to be feared
- explain how Emma's experience shows that change does not need to be feared
- use details from both passages to support your answer

END OF PRACTICE SET

PSSA English Language Arts

Practice Set 19

Reading and Writing

Literary Texts with Writing Tasks

Instructions

This set has two passages for you to read. Read each passage and answer the questions that follow it.

For each multiple-choice question, fill in the circle for the correct answer. For other types of questions, follow the instructions given. Some of the questions require a written answer. Write your answer on the lines provided.

After reading both passages, you will use information from both passages to answer a question. Write your answer on the lines provided.

The Inventor

1) Scott had always been creative. Ever since he had been a child, he had loved to experiment with new ideas. As Scott had grown, his passion had only grown stronger. After attending university, Scott decided that he wanted to become an inventor. He used his studies in engineering to design and produce many brand new things. His friends thought that he was misguided.

2) "You cannot spend your life as an inventor," said his best friend Luke. "You will never have a steady income."

3) Luke worked as a bank manager and worried for his friend's future.

4) "Why don't you reconsider and get a job in the city?" Luke often asked. "You can always invent on the weekends."

5) But Scott would not be distracted from his goals.

6) "This is my dream," he said to Luke. "I have wanted to be an inventor since I was a small child. I am not going to give up."

7) "But you might spend years trying and never make it," Luke said. "You don't want to look back and realize you wasted all your time and talent. You're a great engineer, so you know you could get a good job somewhere and do well for yourself."

8) Scott would explain that he didn't want to work making things that had already been invented. There was no challenge in that. He wanted to use his talents to create something new that would improve how things were done.

9) Luke would shrug and leave his friend to his many different projects. Over several years, Scott developed many ideas that failed to become a success. His first invention was a device that was designed to make a car use less fuel as it traveled. This had many flaws and Scott was unable to sell his invention.

10) His second idea was a special motorcycle helmet that provided better vision for riders. This invention received little support from people who worked in the industry. Scott's friend Luke continued to encourage him to find a different career.

11) "Scott, you have to think about your future. I am proud of you for trying so hard to follow your dreams. I think it is now time to try something else. If you don't, I worry about how things will turn out for you."

12) "Thank you Luke," Scott replied. "I appreciate it. But I cannot stop now. I am so close to coming up with something huge. If I left my designs now, all my life would have been wasted."

13) Luke nodded, "I understand my friend. Just know that I am here to support you."

14) Then one day it happened. Scott completed his design of a new wing for an airplane. It had taken six months. Scott's new invention would improve the efficiency of the plane. He presented it to several companies who all loved his idea. After some competition, a company offered to buy his idea and design plans. Scott accepted the offer.

15) "I knew that one day I would make it!" he said to Luke as they celebrated at his apartment.

16) Luke felt a little guilty for ever suggesting that Scott should give up.

17) "I don't know how you kept going all these years," Luke said. "You definitely deserve every bit of your success."

1 In the sentence below, which word could best be used in place of <u>flaws</u>?

This had many flaws and Scott was unable to sell his invention.

Ⓐ Costs

Ⓑ Faults

Ⓒ Benefits

Ⓓ Uses

2 Read this sentence from the passage.

As Scott had grown, his passion had only grown stronger.

The word <u>passion</u> shows that Scott is very –

Ⓐ enthusiastic

Ⓑ talented

Ⓒ impatient

Ⓓ knowledgeable

3 Which statement best describes how the photograph at the start of the passage relates to the information in the first paragraph?

Ⓐ It shows how Scott loved to experiment with new ideas.

Ⓑ It shows how Scott's passion increased as he got older.

Ⓒ It shows how Scott studied engineering at university.

Ⓓ It shows how Scott's goals were misguided.

4 According to the passage, what did Scott study at college?

- Ⓐ Science
- Ⓑ Mathematics
- Ⓒ Engineering
- Ⓓ Aviation

5 What type of passage is "The Inventor"?

- Ⓐ Realistic fiction
- Ⓑ Science fiction
- Ⓒ Biography
- Ⓓ Fable

6 Complete the table below by listing **two** reasons that Scott gives for continuing to chase his dream of being an inventor and **two** reasons that Luke gives for getting a regular job.

Scott's Reasons for Being an Inventor	Luke's Reasons for Getting a Regular Job

7 The main theme of the passage is about —

- Ⓐ not giving up on your dreams
- Ⓑ making the world a better place
- Ⓒ improving on old ideas
- Ⓓ making time for your friends

8 Based on your answer to Question 7, choose **two** paragraphs that support your answer. On the lines below, explain how each paragraph supports your answer.

Paragraph: _____

_____
_____
_____
_____

Paragraph: _____

_____
_____
_____
_____
_____

9 Which word best describes Scott?

- Ⓐ Foolish
- Ⓑ Determined
- Ⓒ Easygoing
- Ⓓ Sensible

10 Based on your answer to Question 9, give **two** details from the passage that support your answer.

1: _____

_____

2: _____

_____

11 Circle **all** the words from the passage that contain prefixes.

creative	experiment	passion	stronger
university	misguided	reconsider	talent
projects	challenge	improve	different
unable	understand	competition	success

12 The table below describes Scott's inventions and their benefits. Complete the table using details from the passage.

Scott's Inventions

Invention	Benefit of the Invention
Device for a car	Reduced the amount of fuel used
Motorcycle helmet	
New airplane wing	

13 Do you think that Luke is a good friend to Scott? Explain why or why not.

_____

_____

_____

_____

_____

_____

_____

The Aspiring Star

Troy longed to be a professional basketball player. He had loved the sport ever since he was a small child. He was also very skilled and fast on the basketball court. Despite this, he had one small problem. He was very short. His school coach had suggested that he would never make it in the professional leagues. Although he was devastated at first, he refused to give up on his dream.

Troy had several trials at professional clubs but failed to earn a contract. It was then that he attended the training ground of the Los Angeles Lakers. He asked the coach for a trial. As usual, he was refused. It wasn't in his nature just to walk away.

"But you haven't even given me a chance," said Troy.

"Why should I give you a shot?" asked the coach.

Troy paused before he answered.

"Because one day I am going to be the best player in the world and I will be able to help you out," he replied seriously.

The coach smiled at the confidence of the answer.

"Alright kid," he said. "I'll give you a chance to impress me."

Troy took part in a short practice match and was then allowed to showcase his individual skills. He knew he was being given a rare chance and he put everything he had into it. While the other players took a break for water, Troy stayed on the court and showed even more of his ball skills. He was one of the most skillful players on show and had the will to win to match. The coach was stunned.

"You certainly have a lot of talent for a little fellow," he said. "How would you like to sign on a youth contract?"

Troy agreed and was soon rising through the ranks. He was the shortest player by far, but he was also the hardest worker. He felt he had to work hard to overcome the natural height that he lacked. He practiced his ball skills far longer than everyone else. While he couldn't leap as high as everyone else, he was fast and could dribble the ball around everyone. It was rare to see Troy lose the ball or have it stolen from him. He often stole it from other players, and especially those who underestimated him.

Although some players continued to think he was too short to play, they soon changed their minds when they saw him in action. After two short years, he was a regular for the Lakers and had even won the award as the team's most valuable player. Even with Troy's help, the team was struggling. They were not winning many games and there were rumors that the coach was close to losing his job. It was before a game against the New York Jets that he called Troy into his office for a discussion.

"I have heard that if we lose tonight then I will be replaced as coach," he told Troy. "I need you to do more than play well tonight. I need you to carry the team and win the game. Do you remember your promise before I signed you?"

Troy nodded and smiled at his coach.

"You bet I do coach," he replied. "You bet I do."

Troy went on to play the game of his life that evening. The Lakers won the game and won every game that was left that season. The coach kept his job and led his team on to success.

14 Read this sentence from the passage.

> **Although he was devastated at first, he refused to give up on his dream.**

The word <u>devastated</u> means that Troy was —

- Ⓐ understanding
- Ⓑ very upset
- Ⓒ not surprised
- Ⓓ slightly amused

15 Read this sentence from the passage.

> **I need you to carry the team and win the game.**

What does the phrase "carry the team" refer to?

- Ⓐ How Troy will have to cheer on his teammates
- Ⓑ How Troy will have to do extra work
- Ⓒ How Troy will have to motivate the team
- Ⓓ How Troy will have to go against his team

16 What is the main hurdle that makes it difficult for Troy to play at a high level? How does Troy make up for it?

_____

_____

_____

_____

_____

17 Which statement best describes the theme of the passage?

- Ⓐ It is important to keep your promises.
- Ⓑ You can achieve your dreams if you work hard enough.
- Ⓒ Confidence is the key to being great.
- Ⓓ There is no time like the present.

18 In the third paragraph, Troy asks to be given a chance. How does this affect the rest of the events?

- Ⓐ It proves to the coach that Troy is fearless enough to do well.
- Ⓑ It helps Troy understand what it will take to achieve his goal.
- Ⓒ It encourages the coach to be more open-minded about players.
- Ⓓ It allows the coach to see how talented Troy is and get a contract.

19 Read this sentence from the end of the passage spoken by the coach.

Do you remember your promise before I signed you?

What promise is the coach referring to? Explain your answer.

_____

_____

_____

_____

_____

20 What is the point of view in the passage?

- Ⓐ First person
- Ⓑ Second person
- Ⓒ Third person limited
- Ⓓ Third person omniscient

21 How do you think the coach feels about his decision to give Troy a chance at the end of the passage? Use details from the passage to support your answer.

_____

_____

_____

_____

_____

_____

22 Troy's story can be described as inspiring. Explain why Troy's story is inspiring. Use details from the passage in your answer.

_____

_____

_____

_____

_____

_____

23 Complete the web below by listing **three** ways Troy's height actually helped him.

```
            ┌─────────────────┐
            │ The Benefits of │
            │  Troy's Height  │
            └─────────────────┘
           /         |         \
    ┌──────┐    ┌──────┐    ┌──────┐
    │      │    │      │    │      │
    │      │    │      │    │      │
    └──────┘    └──────┘    └──────┘
```

24 Describe **two** examples from the passage that show how Troy takes advantage of every chance he is given.

1: _____

_____

2: _____

_____

25 You have read two passages about people who did not give up on their goals. Write an essay that compares the characters Scott and Troy.

In your response, be sure to
- tell how Scott and Troy both do not give up on their goals
- describe the obstacles they each face
- explain how determination allows Scott and Troy to overcome the obstacles
- use details from both passages to support your answer

END OF PRACTICE SET

PSSA English Language Arts

Practice Set 20

Reading and Writing

Informational Texts with Writing Task

Instructions

This set has three short passages for you to read. Read each passage and answer the questions that follow it.

For each multiple-choice question, fill in the circle for the correct answer. For other types of questions, follow the instructions given. Some of the questions require a written answer. Write your answer on the lines provided.

After reading the three passages, you will use information from all the passages to answer a question. Write your answer on the lines provided.

The Human Skeleton

Did you know that there are over 206 bones in the adult human skeleton? Newborn babies have over 270 bones. As a newborn baby grows, some of their bones are fused together.

The skeleton performs several very important functions within our body. These include providing a support framework, protecting vital organs, and playing a crucial role in the generation of blood cells. Bones are also a storage site for many of the minerals our bodies need. It is important to keep your bones healthy so they can perform all these roles.

Osteoporosis is a medical condition that occurs when the bones become less dense. This makes them weak and brittle, and can lead to bones fracturing easily. When a bone is very brittle, something as simple as coughing can result in a fracture. Osteoporosis can affect anyone, but is most common in women. Luckily, preventing osteoporosis is quite simple. A diet high in calcium and sufficient exercise will usually prevent osteoporosis.

Three Simple Rules

1. Have a Diet High in Calcium
Your body needs calcium to keep your bones strong. Calcium is found in dairy products, leafy green vegetables, and soy products.

2. Get Enough Vitamin D
Your body uses sunlight to make vitamin D. As long as you spend a normal amount of time outdoors, your body should be getting enough vitamin D. Vitamin D is also found in salmon, tuna, and eggs.

3. Exercise
Regular exercise will keep your bones strong and healthy. Walking, running, jogging, or playing sports are all good for the health of your bones.

1. Choose **two** of the words below that are used in the passage. Explain how you can tell what each word chosen means by how it is used in the passage.

        fused   brittle   fracture   sufficient

Word 1: _____

_____

_____

_____

Word 2: _____

_____

_____

_____

2. Which two words from the passage have about the same meaning?
   - Ⓐ   *storage, minerals*
   - Ⓑ   *sunlight, outdoors*
   - Ⓒ   *adult, newborn*
   - Ⓓ   *vital, crucial*

3 Complete the web below using information from the passage.

```
┌──────────────────┐                    ┌──────────────────┐
│  being a support │                    │                  │
│    framework     │                    │                  │
└──────────────────┘                    └──────────────────┘
              \                        /
               \    ┌──────────────┐  /
                \   │ Functions of │ /
                 ───│     the      │──
                /   │   Skeleton   │  \
               /    └──────────────┘   \
              /                         \
┌──────────────────┐                    ┌──────────────────┐
│                  │                    │                  │
│                  │                    │                  │
└──────────────────┘                    └──────────────────┘
```

4 According to the passage, how are adults different from children?

　Ⓐ　They have more bones.

　Ⓑ　They have fewer bones.

　Ⓒ　Their bones have more purposes.

　Ⓓ　Their bones have fewer purposes.

5 What is the main reason the author begins the passage with a question?

　Ⓐ　To present a fact in a way that creates interest in the topic

　Ⓑ　To explain the main purpose of the article

　Ⓒ　To suggest that many people do not realize the importance of the skeleton

　Ⓓ　To encourage readers to research and find out more about the human skeleton

6 Which detail from the passage did you find most interesting or surprising? Explain why you found that detail interesting or surprising.

_____

_____

_____

_____

_____

7 What is the main purpose of the section titled "Three Simple Rules"? In your answer, explain how these rules relate to the rest of the passage.

_____

_____

_____

_____

_____

Food Poisoning

Bacteria grow quickly in the right conditions. When food isn't prepared, kept, or handled properly it has the potential to make you very ill. Food poisoning occurs when bacteria are introduced into food before it is eaten. Food poisoning can sometimes be as mild as having a stomachache, but it can also be much more serious. The Centers for Disease Control and Prevention (CDC) states that almost 50 million Americans get food poisoning every year. Of those, around 125,000 people are admitted to hospital and there are around 3,000 deaths. Luckily, food poisoning can be prevented. All you have to do is follow a few simple rules.

1: Wash your hands and the equipment you're going to use to prepare and serve the food.

2: Don't use the same chopping board for meat that you use to prepare fruit and vegetables. This is especially important if the fruit and vegetables are served raw.

3: Ensure your food is cooked thoroughly. The cooking process destroys most harmful bacteria, so this step can prevent food poisoning even when the raw food contains bacteria.

4: Properly store your food.

5: Make sure your refrigerator temperature is set low enough.

6: Follow the directions on packaging for how to store foods once they are open, and for how long to store food for.

7: Don't unfreeze and then refreeze food.

Top Tip

Many foods have to be used within a few days once they've been opened. It can be easy to forget when something was opened. Keep a marker near the fridge and write on the packaging what date the food was opened.

8 In rule 3, which word could best be used in place of <u>thoroughly</u>?

  Ⓐ Quickly

  Ⓑ Completely

  Ⓒ Cleanly

  Ⓓ Nicely

9 Which rule does the information in the box mainly relate to? Circle the answer you have chosen.

            1   2   3   4   5   6   7

10 Based on your answer to Question 9, describe why you chose that rule. In your answer, explain how the rule and the information in the box relate to each other.

_____

_____

_____

_____

_____

11 What is the main purpose of the first paragraph?

Ⓐ To describe how to prevent food poisoning

Ⓑ To explain the importance of food safety

Ⓒ To encourage people to cook their own food

Ⓓ To show that bacteria can grow anywhere

12 Which of these rules from the passage best supports the conclusion that bacteria grow poorly in cold conditions?

Ⓐ *Don't use the same chopping board for chopping meat that you use to prepare fruit and vegetables.*

Ⓑ *Ensure your food is cooked thoroughly.*

Ⓒ *Make sure your refrigerator temperature is set low enough.*

Ⓓ *Don't unfreeze and then refreeze food.*

13 Describe **two** details the author includes to show the seriousness of food poisoning.

1: _____

_____

2: _____

_____

14 What is the cause of food poisoning? Use details from the passage to support your answer.

_____

_____

_____

_____

_____

15 Why do you think it is important not to use the same chopping board for meat that you use for fruit and vegetables? Explain your answer.

_____

_____

_____

_____

_____

Take a Deep Breath

The lung is an organ that is used to help many living things breathe. Humans have two lungs in their body. The lungs have several important purposes. The main purpose of the lungs is to take in oxygen from the air. Carbon dioxide leaves the body via the lungs. The lungs are also used to protect the heart from any sudden shocks to the chest. Another purpose of the lungs is to filter blood clots.

Looking After the Lungs

It is important to take good care of your lungs. One of the best ways to keep your lungs healthy is to exercise often. This gives your lungs a workout! The more you exercise, the stronger your lungs will become!

The lungs are so important that your body has built-in ways of protecting them. Have you ever breathed in dust? What happened? Have you heard of people who are affected by pollen in the air? If there is anything getting into the body from the air, your body has special ways of dealing with it. One way is to cough, which removes particles from the lungs and breathing passages. The other way is to sneeze, which removes particles from the nasal cavity and nose.

Sneezing is a bodily reflex similar to a cough. It serves the same purpose of a cough, which is to remove foreign bodies and irritants from the body. However, a sneeze is much more powerful than a cough. In fact, the air leaving the body from a sneeze can travel at speeds of up to 100 miles per hour!

A sneeze occurs when air is rapidly expelled, or removed from, the lungs. The scientific term for sneezing is sternutation. There are four main reasons that people sneeze.

- Irritation – people sneeze when something irritates the nose. This is the body's way of cleaning the nose and stopping irritants from getting into the lungs.
- Light – people can sneeze when they are suddenly exposed to bright light.
- Feeling full – some people have a very rare condition where they sneeze as a response to feeling very full after a meal.
- Infection – many infections by viruses, including the common cold, can cause people to sneeze. The purpose of the sneeze is to remove virus particles from the body.

The most common reason people sneeze is due to irritation. Many people sneeze when they breathe in dust, pollen, or other irritants. This condition is known as hay fever, and is most common in spring when there is a lot of pollen in the air.

For some people, spring flowers are a wonderful sign that the cold weather of winter and fall has passed. For others, flowers means the beginning of hay fever season.

16 Which sentence states the main idea of the first paragraph?

  Ⓐ Humans have two lungs in their body.

  Ⓑ The lungs have several important purposes.

  Ⓒ Carbon dioxide leaves the body via the lungs.

  Ⓓ Another purpose of the lungs is to filter blood clots.

17 What is the main purpose of the information in the box?

  Ⓐ To give advice on how to have healthy lungs

  Ⓑ To describe one of the purposes of the lungs

  Ⓒ To describe the two human lungs

  Ⓓ To show that lungs are important organs

18 Select **all** the statements below that are purposes of the lungs.

  ☐ Taking in oxygen

  ☐ Storing minerals

  ☐ Removing carbon dioxide

  ☐ Protecting the heart

  ☐ Filtering blood clots

  ☐ Making energy

19 How is the paragraph below mainly organized?

> **Sneezing is a bodily reflex similar to a cough. It serves the same purpose of a cough, which is to remove foreign bodies and irritants from the body. However, a sneeze is much more powerful than a cough. In fact, the air leaving the body from a sneeze can travel at speeds of up to 100 miles per hour!**

- Ⓐ A problem is described and then a solution is given.
- Ⓑ Events are described in the order they occur.
- Ⓒ Facts are given to support an argument.
- Ⓓ Two events are compared.

20 The photograph at the end of the passage mainly relates to which cause of sneezing?
- Ⓐ Irritation
- Ⓑ Light
- Ⓒ Feeling full
- Ⓓ Infection

21 How does the diagram help show how sneezing would clean the nose?
- Ⓐ It shows how the lungs can hold a lot of air.
- Ⓑ It shows how air only moves in one direction.
- Ⓒ It shows how quickly the air would be traveling.
- Ⓓ It shows how air from the lungs would travel through the nose.

22 Rank the following causes of sneezing from most common to least common. Write 1, 2, 3, and 4 on the lines to show your choices.

___ Irritation

___ Light

___ Feeling full

___ Infection

23 Which term best describes the sentence below?

The scientific term for sneezing is sternutation.

Ⓐ Comparison

Ⓑ Definition

Ⓒ Exaggeration

Ⓓ Assumption

24 Describe **two** ways that sneezing is different from coughing.

1: _____

_____

2: _____

_____

25 You have read three passages that relate to being healthy. The passages show how your body tries to keep you healthy and how you can keep healthy. Write an article for your school newspaper encouraging students to be healthy.

In your response, be sure to
- describe how your body works to keep you healthy
- explain why it is important to help your body do its job
- describe what people can do to help stay healthy
- use details from the three passages to support your answer

END OF PRACTICE SET

Made in the USA
Middletown, DE
26 February 2025